Practical Anarchy

Practical Anarchy

THE FREEDOM OF THE FUTURE

• • •

Stefan Molyneux

ISBN: 1975654323
ISBN 13: 9781975654320

Contents

Preface

· · ·

Despite our universal abhorrence, evils continue to plague the world, without respite. We fear and hate war, yet war continues. Our souls revolt against unjust imprisonment and torture, yet such injustices continue. We feel powerless in the face of endless tax increases – and with good reason. We feel agonizing compassion for those who are caught up in the endless bloody nets of tribal conflicts, condemned to mute horror and blank-eyed starvation. The plight of the enslaved weighs down our hearts with the rusty chains of useless sympathy. We would do almost *anything* to free the world from such monstrous evils – yet we feel so helpless! We all want a free and wonderful world, and yet feel utterly paralyzed before these monsters who commit such universal crimes...

Violence, injustice and brutal control are truly the malignant cancers of our species. Philosophers have chided and reasoned in vain for thousands of years. Governments have been instituted to serve and protect the people – yet always escape the flimsy walls of their paper prisons and spread their choking powers across society, darkening hope and the future.

In this book, I do my part to put an end to these evils.

I know exactly how all these horrors can be ended.

I am fully aware of the outlandishness of this claim. I am fully aware that you have every right to be perfectly skeptical and cynical about the contents of this book. I would not blame you at all if you laughed in my face, spat at my feet – did anything that you pleased – as long as I could get you to turn just one more page.

Because – what if it *were* possible?

What if it *were* possible to live in a world free of the terror and genocide of war? What if it *were* possible to live in a world without unjust imprisonment, institutionalized rape, and the endless subjugation of the helpless and arming of the vicious and evil?

What if you held in your hands a small blueprint that could lead to just such a world? A world of peace and plenty – of compassion, voluntarism, virtue and true liberty?

Isn't that what we all really dream of?

Isn't that the world that we wish with all our hearts that our children could inherit?

Isn't that the world that we would like to take even a *few* steps towards?

We can get there.

Why do we examine the destination before mapping the journey?

Nietzsche said, "He who has a *why*... can bear with almost any *how*."

Before we discuss how to get to freedom, why must know why a stateless society is so essential.

This book will show you what *real* freedom looks like.

PART 1

Methodology

• • •

INTRODUCTION

THE INEVITABLE – AND HIGHLY intelligent – questions that arose in response to my last book "Everyday Anarchy" mostly centered on the question of how a stateless society could self-organize in practical terms.

Naturally, these sorts of questions are a fascinating and endless kind of intellectual delight. Much as Alice mused as she fell down the hole at the beginning of Lewis Carroll's famous book, we intellectuals are tempted to design the future down to the last detail. We try to respond to every conceivable objection with yet another essay on how roads can be delivered in the absence of a government, or how international treaties can work in the absence of law courts, or how children can be protected in the absence of the police, or how national defense can be secured in the absence of a State army, and how the poor can receive an education in the absence of public schools, and how and why doctors will help the impoverished sick without being forced to, and so on.

I have always argued that these answers – though intellectually stimulating and enjoyably debatable – will never convince those who wish to avoid the morality and practicality of nonviolent solutions to the problems of social organization.

For instance, in my last book, as well as a recent video, I provided a proof for anarchy, which relied on the reality of non-contractual special-interest group relationships with up-and-coming politicians. A large number of people wrote to me in response, saying either that such special interest relationships did not exist – surely a laughable proposition, given the 30,000 plus lobbyists registered in Washington, DC alone – or that if I wanted anarchy, and democracy was a great proof of the practical functionality of anarchy, then surely I should be happy with democracy!

There seems to be no end to the foolish statements that can be uttered by those afraid of the truth. The truth, as Socrates gave his life to show, remains highly threatening to entrenched interests and has a very personal and volatile effect on our immediate relationships.

In reality, it is not so much a stateless society that we fear, but rather a family-less and friendless society where we rock gently, hugging our useless truths to our chests; solitary, ostracized, alone, rejected, scorned, derided. The truth is a desert island, we fear, and so as evolutionarily social animals, we join our corrupt circles in mocking and attacking the truth, and resent those who tell the truth, for revealing the corruption that formerly was only visible unconsciously – which is to say, largely invisible.

It is important to understand up front that this book will contain truths that will likely be highly threatening to you – and certainly to those around you. The world, viewed philosophically, remains a series of slave camps, where citizens – tax livestock – labor under the chains of illusion in the service of their masters. As I talked about in my book, "Real-Time Relationships," the predations of the rulers survive on the horizontal attacks of the slaves. Because we savage each other, we remain ruled by savages.

Thus, you may find that as you read this book, you experience a rising frustration and irritation with its contents – and possibly with me as well, if experience is any guide.

I certainly do sympathize with these emotions, and truly understand their cause, but I would strongly urge you to refrain from sending me angry e-mails – for your sake, not mine. It is, as you know, highly unjust to attack a truth teller for the discomfort he causes.

It is not my fault that you have been lied to your whole life long.

Furthermore, the lies exist whether or not you hear the truth – from me, or from anyone else.

LIMITATIONS

It is impossible for any single man – or group of men – to ever design or predict all the details of any society. In order for you to get the most out of this book, I will make a few suggestions which may be helpful.

First of all, if you approach this book with the idea that you're going to find every possible gap in an argument, or nook and cranny where uncertainty may reside, then this book will be a complete waste of time, and will raise your blood pressure for absolutely no purpose whatsoever.

When Adam Smith formulated the arguments for the free market in the late 18th century, it was not considered a requirement that he predict the stock price of IBM in 1961. He began working with a number of observable and empirical principles, and proved them with rational arguments and well-known examples.

The validity of the "invisible hand" was not dependent upon Adam Smith predicting and describing in detail the invention of, say, the Internet. The methods that free men and women invent and use to solve social problems cannot reasonably be predicted in advance, and finding every conceivable fault with any and all such possible predictions is arguing against a mere theoretical possibility, which is both futile and ridiculous.

That having been said, it is still worth reviewing some possible solutions to social organization that do not involve the monopolistic violence of the State. When Enlightenment thinkers attacked and undermined the exploitive illusions of religion, they were not able to provide a valid and scientific system of ethics to replace the mad moral commandments of historical superstition. It certainly is valuable to disprove existing "truths," but if we do not come up with at least plausible alternatives, these falsehoods inevitably tend to morph and reemerge in a different form. Thus did the death of religion give rise to totalitarianism – just another worship of an abstract and irrational moral absolute; the "State" rather than a "god." The unjust aristocratic privileges of the minority that the Founding Fathers so railed against simply morphed into the unjust privileges of the majority in the form of "mob rule" democracy – which then morphed back into the unjust aristocratic privileges of the minority in the form of a political ruling class.

Men and societies all need rules to live by, and if existing rules get knocked down, they simply rise again in another form if rational replacements are not provided. Exposing a lie simply breeds different lies, unless the truth is also advanced.

I have set myself a number of goals in the writing of this book that I wanted to mention up front, so you could understand the approach that I am taking – the strengths and weaknesses of what I am up to, as it were.

First, I promise to refrain from exhausting your patience by trying to come up with every conceivable solution to every conceivable problem. Not only would this end up being grindingly boring, but it would also indicate a strange kind of intellectual insecurity, and an unwillingness to give you the respect of accepting that you can very easily think for yourself about the solutions to the problems discussed in this book. My aim is to give you a framework for thinking about these issues, rather than have you sit passively as I explicate the widest variety of solutions to all conceivable problems.

In other words, my purpose in this book is to teach you to be a mathematician, not show you how good a mathematician I am.

Teaching you how to solve problems is far more respectful than giving you solutions. I have always said that everyone is a genius, and everyone is a philosopher. You do not need me to spell out how a stateless society can work in every detail, but rather to give you a framework which you can use to work out your own answers, and satisfy yourself how well a truly free society will work.

When Francis Bacon was putting forward the scientific method in the 16th century, it was not necessary for him to solve every conceivable scientific problem in order to prove the value of his methodology. It certainly was useful for him to show how his methodology had solved a number of vexing problems, and that it pointed the way to answers in a number of other areas, but of course if Bacon had been able to solve every conceivable scientific problem that could ever possibly arise, there would be precious little need for his scientific method at all, since we would just consult his writings whenever we had a scientific problem that we could not solve.

In the same way, as a philosopher I am interested in teaching people how to think in a new way, rather than giving them explicit answers to every conceivable problem. My approach to rational and scientific ethics – Universally Preferable Behavior (UPB) – is to provide people a framework for evaluating moral propositions, rather than to give them an utterly finalized system of ethics. If such a system of ethics ever could be developed – which seems highly unlikely, given the inevitably-changing conditions of life, society and technology – then no one would ever have to think about ethics ever again, and philosophy would fall into the abyss reserved for dead religions and defunct ideologies, interesting only as yet another example of a temporary historical illusion, like the worship of Zeus or Mussolini or Paris Hilton.

The scientific method certainly did – and does – provide an objective methodology for gaining valid knowledge and understanding of the physical world, just as UPB provides an objective methodology for separating truth from falsehood when it comes to evaluating moral propositions, and the free market provides an objective methodology for determining value in the provision of goods and services, through the mechanism of price.

The value of the scientific method only truly becomes apparent when we abandon religious or superstitious revelation as a valid source of "truth." We only refer to a compass when we become uncertain of our direction. We only begin to develop science when we start to doubt religion. We only begin to accept the validity of the free market when we doubt the ethics and practicality of coercive central planning. On a more personal level, we only begin to change our approach to relationships when we at last begin to suspect that we *ourselves* may be the source of our problems.

Much like a river, alternative tributaries only arise when the original flow is blocked. The development of new paradigms in thought is in general more *provoked* than plotted, and erupts from a rising exasperation with the falsehoods of existing "solutions." This spike in emotion can sometimes arise with extraordinary rapidity, from a slow build to a sudden explosion – and it is my belief that this is where we are poised in the present when it comes to an examination of the use of violence in solving social problems.

As a vivid, living value, the nation-state as an object of worship and a source of practical and moral solutions is as dead as King Tutankhamun. No one truly believes anymore that the State can solve the problems of poverty, of mis-education, of war, of ill health, of security for the aged and so on. Governments are now viewed with extraordinary suspicion and cynicism. It is true that many people still believe that the *idea* of government can somehow be rescued, but there is an extraordinary level of exasperation, frustration and anxiety with our existing methods of solving social problems. When someone says that we need yet *another* government program to "solve" all the problems created or exacerbated by previous government programs, most people now view this approach as an eye-rolling non-answer.

Of course, we still hear a lot about government "solutions" in the media, academia, and the arts, but most people now understand – at least emotionally – that this bleating arises from special interest groups that are either threatened or protected by the State – the automatic reaction of "increase regulation!" When a problem arises, this demand no longer comes from the people, but rather from those parties that will benefit from increased regulation.

The rise of the Internet has also rocked the mainstream paradigm of "government as virtue." In particular, the US-led invasion of Iraq has contributed to a final collapse in belief about the virtue of statist solutions to complex problems. It is easier to believe the lies of the past, since we were not there when they were told – it is harder to believe in the lies of the present, since we can see them unraveling before our very eyes.

Thus, our belief that the government can solve problems is collapsing on two fronts – first, we now understand that the government *cannot* solve problems – and second, and more importantly, we can see that the government *is not giving up any of its control over the problems it so obviously cannot solve.*

This last point is worth expanding upon, since it is so important, and so often overlooked.

If the government claims to take our money in order to solve the problem of poverty, for instance, but the government clearly does *not* solve the problem of poverty, but rather in fact tends to make it worse, what then do we begin to understand when the government continues to take our money?

If I take your money telling you that I will ship you an iPod, what realization do you come to when I neither ship you the iPod nor return your money?

Surely you understand that I only promised you the iPod in order to steal your money.

In the same way, the government did not increase our taxes in order to solve the problem of poverty, but rather claimed that it wanted to solve the problem of poverty in order to increase our taxes. This is the only way to explain the basic fact that the problem of poverty has not been solved – and in fact is worse now – but the government continues to increase our taxes.

We are all beginning to understand – at least at an unconscious level – that the government lies to us about helping others in order to take our money.

The Answer?

If religion is not the answer, and the State is not the answer, then what is?

Well, when a particular "answer" has proven so universally disastrous, the first place to look is the opposite of that answer.

If "no property rights" (communism) is disastrous, then "property rights" (free markets) are most likely to be beneficial.

If faith is disastrous, then science is most likely to be beneficial.

If superstition is disastrous, than reason and evidence are most likely to be beneficial.

If violence is disastrous, then peace and negotiation are most likely to be beneficial.

If the State is disastrous, then *anarchism* is most likely to be beneficial.

It is this last statement that tends to be the most challenging for people.

Many of us can accept a world without gods and devils, without heaven and hell, without original sin and imaginary redemption – but we cannot accept, or even imagine, a world without governments.

Many of us can picture a world with a minimum government – with a State concerned only with law courts, police and the military – but we cannot picture a world without a government at all.

A Christian can accept a world where 9,999 gods are ridiculous and false illusions, but that *his* God – the God of the Old Testament – is a true, real and living deity. A Christian remains an atheist with regards to almost every god, but becomes an utter theist with regards to his own deity. Getting rid of almost all gods is utterly sensible – getting rid of that one final God is utterly incomprehensible.

In the same way, Libertarians, Objectivists and other minarchists feel that getting rid of 99% of existing government functions is utterly moral – but getting rid of that last 1% is utterly *immoral!*

We do not accept these reservations in other areas of our lives, which is enough to make us suspicious of the true motives behind such statements. A woman who is beaten up only once a month lives 99.99% of her life violence-free, but we would not consider her beatings acceptable on that ground. It would be even more ridiculous to say that a woman should not be beaten every day, but that it would be utterly immoral to also suggest that she should not be beaten at *all*.

If I claim that it is moral to reduce State violence, can I claim that it is utterly immoral to eliminate such violence completely? Can I dedicate my life to reducing the incidence of cancer, but then claim that eliminating cancer completely would be utterly immoral? Can I reasonably set up a charity to reduce poverty, but then claim in my mission statement that the elimination of poverty would be a dire evil?

Of course not – I would be viewed as an irrational lunatic at best for making such statements.

Those who claim that a *reduction* of violence is a moral ideal, but who then also claim that the *elimination* of violence would be a moral evil, must at least recognize, if they wish to retain any credibility, that they are proposing an entirely foolish contradiction.

By "violence" here, I do not mean that anarchism will completely eliminate human violence – the violence that I am talking about here is the morally "justified" and institutionalized initiation of force that is the foundation of State power. (I am not going to go into a lengthy discussion here about the nature of the State, or the moral reasoning against the initiation of violence, since I have dealt with those topics at length in my podcasts, and in other books. Suffice to say that the State is by definition a group of individuals who claim the right to initiate the use of force against legally-disarmed citizens in a specific geographical region.)

Thus, I think it is reasonable for us to take the approach that if it *were* possible to run society without a government, this would be a massive net positive.

When we have governments, we inevitably get wars, politically motivated and unjust laws, the incarceration of nonviolent "criminals," the over-printing of money and the resulting inflation, the enslavement of future generations through immoral deficits, the mis-education of the young, rampant vote buying, endless tax increases, arms sales around the world, unjust subsidies to specific industries, economic and practical inefficiencies of every conceivable kind, the creation of permanent underclasses through welfare and illegal immigration, vast increases in the power and violence of organized crime through restrictions on drugs, prostitution and gambling – the list of State crimes is virtually endless.

When we choose to justify governments, we inevitably choose to justify the crimes of those in power. Choosing government is also choosing war, genocide, enslavement, financial, moral and educational corruption, propaganda, the spread of violence and so on.

You can never get one without the other. Imagining otherwise is like imagining that you can choose to justify the Mafia without also justifying the violence that it uses to maintain its power. We may as well imagine that we can support the troops without simultaneously supporting the murders they commit.

Given the number of bloody and genocidal crimes that orbit the power of the State, surely we can at least be open to the possibility that society can be organized far more effectively and morally without such an evil power at its center. If it turns out that society *can* run without a State – even haltingly, even imperfectly – then surely we should accept such practical imperfections for the sake of avoiding such rampant and bottomless crimes against humanity. Surely, even if anarchy were proven to produce fewer and worse roads, we could accept some mildly inconvenient and bumpy rides for the sake of releasing billions of people from direct or indirect enslavement to their political masters.

To analogize this, imagine that someone in the 19th century proved that cotton would be 10% rougher if slavery were abolished. Would it be moral or reasonable for people to say, "Well, it is certainly true that slavery is a great evil, but I still prefer it to slightly less comfortable cotton!"?

No, we would view such monstrous selfishness as staggeringly corrupt. The moral hypocrisy of claiming to be against slavery, but refusing to actually *oppose* slavery for fear of even the mildest practical inconvenience, would be an ethical evil that would be hard to comprehend.

Thus, when people dismiss the possibility of anarchy out of hand by saying, "Oh, but how would roads be provided?" what they are *really* saying is that they support war, genocide, tax enslavement and the incarceration and rape of the innocent, because they themselves cannot imagine how roads might be provided in the absence of violence. "People should be murdered, raped and imprisoned because I am concerned that the roads I use might be slightly less convenient." Can anyone look at the moral horror of this statement without feeling a bottomless and existential nausea?

Now, imagine that the reality of the situation is that roads will be provided far more efficiently and productively in a stateless society?

If *that* is the case, then the practical considerations turn out to be the complete opposite of the truth – that we are accepting murder, genocide and rape for the sake of *bad* roads, rather than good roads!

This kind of net loss provides the moral and rational core of the arguments in favor of a stateless society. While it is certainly true that some people will end up losing out under anarchy, it is the evil and corrupt who will lose the most, just as priests lose out in an atheistic society, much to the relief of children everywhere. The true reality of an anarchic society is that the moral goals of every reasonable human being – the alleviation of poverty, the provision of "public services," the education of the young, the protection of children, the old and the infirm, will actually be created and provided in a positive, productive, gentle and moral manner.

The great lie of the statist society is that the helpless and dependent are protected, when in fact they are trapped and exploited.

The great lie of the statist society is that the ignorant are educated, when in fact they are made even more ignorant.

The great truth of the anarchic society is that the helpless are protected, the ignorant are educated, the sick are treated – and that roads are built, and are better.

To gain the beauty and virtue of anarchism, we sacrifice nothing but our illusions.

Surely, we should actually want to help people, rather than just pretend that we are doing so.

Surely, we should not sacrifice the peace of the world to our fears of imperfect roads.

The Argument from Apocalypse

Of course, people do not say that we should not live in a free society because the roads might be imperfect. The endless argument against anarchism is the "Argument from Apocalypse." (AFA)

The AFA is not an argument at all, of course, but rather relies on rampant fear mongering, and an argument from intimidation.

Basically, the argument goes something like this:

"We're all gonna DIEEEEEEE!"

It would actually be nice if it were slightly more sophisticated than that, but the reality is that it is not.

The basic argument is that if we accept proposition "X," civilized society will collapse, children will die in the streets, the old will end up eating each other, and the world will dissolve into an endless and apocalyptic war of all against all.

This is not an argument at all, since it relies on fear and intimidation. Darwin faced exactly the same "objections" when he first published his theory of evolution. "If we accept that we are descended from apes, everybody will abandon morality, society will collapse, war of all against all etc etc etc."

Abolitionists faced the same argument when suggesting that slavery should be abolished; atheists face the same silly objections when disproving the existence of God; philosophers have been put to death for suggesting that ethics should be based on something other than superstition; scientists are accused of the same evils whenever some new development threatens people's existing prejudices – it is all the most rampant nonsense, which survives only because of its endless effectiveness.

The AFA remains effective because of a basic logical fallacy which has doubtless been around since the dawn of speech: "Belief 'X' would result in immorality or destruction, and so only a fool or an evil man would advocate 'X'."

Since very few people wish to appear either foolish or evil, they tend to back down in the face of this argument, or take the imprudent path – which I have trod many a time – of attempting to disprove the AFA.

"Anarchism results in evil!" cometh the cry – and anarchists around the world endlessly respond with: "No it won't!" – thus losing the argument before it even begins.

The only thing that is relevant in any intellectual argument is whether it is true or not. Refusing to examine the validity and consistency of a mathematical argument because you fear that accepting its conclusions will result in endless evil is simply surrendering to superstitious fear-mongering, and abandoning your rationality. Propositions cannot be evil – mathematics cannot be evil – statism cannot be evil – error cannot be evil – and the truth is not virtuous!

A proposition cannot strangle a baby; an argument cannot rape a nun, and a theory of anarchism cannot turn people into shrunken-headed zombies in hot pursuit of Will Smith.

A theory of anarchism can only be true or false, valid or invalid, logical or illogical.

If someone deploys the AFA, it proves nothing except that he has no good arguments, and that the proposition in front of him is emotionally unsettling in some way. In other words, all that the AFA proves is intellectual idiocy and emotional immaturity. It is the philosophical equivalent of arguing against the proposition that "ice cream contains milk," by saying, "I once had a dream that an ice cream monster was trying to *eat me!*" It is the kind of *non sequitur* we would expect from a very young child, which would only indicate an utter incomprehension of the proposed statement.

People who are threatened by ideas should at least have the honesty to say, "I am threatened by this idea," rather than pretend that the idea is somehow objectively threatening to the human race as a whole. If I am afraid of short men, I should be honest about my fears and say, "I am afraid of short men," rather than vehemently argue that short men will somehow destroy the world!

However, prejudice against anarchists – much like prejudice against atheists – is one of the last remaining acceptable bigotries in the world. We cannot judge any group negatively – except a group that relies on reason, evidence and nonviolence.

Thus, it will not do us any good to run screaming from the idea of a stateless society, imagining all kinds of demonic horrors. If we allow fear-mongering to not only inform, but rather define and direct our thinking, then we are left without the ability to think at all, but instead must sit clutching the skirts of those who tell us tall and terrifying tales.

We cannot judge the truth of an idea by our fears of its effect.

Arguments for or against the existence of gods are not validated by our fears of – or desires for – a godless universe. We cannot oppose a theory of gravity by saying that it is unpleasant to fall down stairs; neither can we oppose a new theory by demanding prior historical examples. The entire point of a new theory is that it is unprecedented; the first man to invent a jet aircraft could scarcely submit examples of jet aircraft flying in the past.

Another common objection to anarchic theories is that they are not embraced or validated by professional intellectuals, philosophers and academics.

This is very true, and, as I explained in great detail in my book, "Everyday Anarchy," I think we can view this as a positive, rather than a negative.

Still, is it reasonable for me to ask you to reject the near-universal consensus of highly intelligent people – professors, pundits, columnists, academics and so on – simply because they happen to disagree with or ignore the propositions that I am putting forward here? Surely we have all heard of a number of scam artists – particularly on the Internet – who sell snake oil solutions to genuine ailments, preying upon the weak, the desperate and the gullible. Is it reasonable to ask everyone to completely abandon respect for scholarship and professionalism, to turf experts for the sake of their own preferred opinions? Is this not our fear of what the Internet will do to social consensus? Can we not find on the Wild West of the Web articles claiming that smoking is good for you, that space aliens were responsible for 9/11, that exercise is dangerous, fluoride will kill you and eating fat will make you lose weight?

How can we be sure that a theory of anarchism is not just another one of these crackpot ideas that rails against the universal consensus of experts in the field, attempting to dislodge sober scholarship with wild-eyed speculation? Perhaps this book is just a form of elaborate trickery, a playing out of some wretched and buried psychological trauma, designed to separate you from your friends and family by infecting you with strange and illicit ideas – and taking your money to boot, since Freedomain Radio relies on voluntary donations!

Of course, these are all excellent questions to ask, and I for one would be highly unlikely to pit my own judgment against that of, say, my doctor or my accountant. One of the main reasons that we need specialists is because enormous swaths of human knowledge remain buried under entirely counterintuitive paradigms. Who would have thought that making your gums bleed – at least at first – with floss would lead to oral health? Exercise often feels bad, and eating pie always feels very good, and so we need experts to remind us of the long-term effects of such activities, compared to the short-term incentives and disincentives. We prefer to spend money in the moment rather than save it for a rainy day; a surgeon might make us feel very unwell in order to prevent or cure an illness that we may not have even felt yet; a friend might strive to impress upon us the emotional problems of a highly attractive sexual partner; and the dark satisfactions of discharging anger towards a spouse in the present might create for us a very unpleasant future indeed.

In all these areas, we rely on the objectivity and expertise of those around us, who possess the training and knowledge to steer us against our immediate desires, or who are not subject to our own immediate desires – as in the case of our friends – and so can often see things more clearly.

What about the famous idea that deep study tends to lead to moderation? A little learning is a dangerous thing, it is often said – and with good reason. If we are ignorant of the effects of early childhood experiences and the long-term effects on the psychology of the personality, it is far easier to look at criminals as simply "bad guys." If we are ignorant of the basic truth that history is almost always a tale told by those in power in order to justify and support their own "virtue," then we shall inevitably be genuinely shocked when we come across the long-lost truths of the vanquished, or the foreign – or the dead.

Thus, should we not look for moderation in our responses to complex questions? The problem of health is complex, requiring a wide variety of inputs from nutritionists, physical trainers, doctors, psychologists and so on – most of whom will counsel a form of Aristotelian moderation. Too little exercise leads to brittle bones and flab; too much exercise leads to injury. Too little food leads to a lack of energy; too much food leads to excess weight. An over-focus on the desires and needs of others leads to codependency; too little focus leads to selfish narcissism. Parents must often attempt to strike a balance between discipline and indulgence; the needs of the many must be balanced with the needs of the few, even in just the business arena; the sacrifice of our own short-term happiness for the sake of the longer-term happiness of another we love is all part and parcel of having a wise, flourishing and positive set of personal and professional relationships.

Given all this complexity, does the answer of "just get rid of the government!" not strike us as overly simplistic? My mother used to talk about three spheres within society – business, government and labor – and the need to find a balance between them. "The endless challenge in society is finding a way to stimulate business growth – but not at the expense of labor – so that there is enough tax revenue for government to provide effective social services."

This kind of juggling act strikes us as eminently mature in many ways, and recognizes that, just as there is good and bad in every individual, so there is good and bad in every group. You can find bad and corrupt people in the realm of politics, labor and business, if you want – but stretching this basic reality into an outright condemnation of any group seems explicitly prejudicial. A man who has been robbed by a Chinese acrobat would scarcely be justified in demanding that the world be utterly rid of Chinese acrobats. One swallow does not a summer make; nor do bad politicians invalidate the value of government as a whole.

Furthermore, isn't it rather childish to suggest that we rid ourselves of an institution that is so open and responsive to our feedback? We live in a democracy, for heaven's sake – why throw the baby out with the bathwater, when we can get involved and change the system? If we do not like a particular company's business practices, we do not have to throw out "capitalism" as a whole – we can inform others about their odious practices, organize boycotts and so on. Surely the communicative power of the Internet has removed significant barriers to freedom of self-expression and the exchange of information, to the point where we no longer need to sit back when an institution fails to serve us, but rather we can very quickly and effectively work to bring about change in our political system.

It also seems very alarming for us to take the enormous risk of getting rid of a government. Such a radical step has never been taken before as part of a conscious philosophical program. Governments have collapsed, of course – and we can only look at the example of Somalia to see the infighting and warlords that can arise from such a situation – and governments have been taken over, either internally or externally – but there is no example in history of consciously dismantling a State without any goal of replacing it. Does it seem sensible to go directly against the entire collective history of our species, and throw out an essential human institution that has been around as long as we have? Other radical "reorganizations" of human society have resulted in endless slaughter, chaos, war, and the staggering disorientation of children raised without families, of rampant polygamy, communal "ownership" and so on. It does seem to be a particular curse of our species that every generation or two, some new idea comes along which aims to overthrow the entire history of human interaction, and replace the controlled hurly-burly of a State-managed free market with something like fascism, socialism or communism. Then, some other wild-eyed rebel comes along and decries that, "family is dictatorship," and attempts to undermine and destroy that most essential component of social life, the nuclear family. Then someone else comes along and says, "Property is theft!" and the cycle just seems to start all over again.

The basics of human society – of human life itself – seem to be that families are good, that private property is important, that the greed of the free market cannot provide all possible goods and services, that some form of centralized regulation and law-making seems to be essential, that there is good and bad in everyone, but there are some very good people, and some very bad people, and that the good people need a government to protect them from the bad people.

I confess that it must be quite exasperating for people to hear some of the basics that are so commonly accepted as truths opened up once more for a new examination. Perhaps it feels somewhat akin to a biologist being lectured to by a creationist during a long intercontinental flight, or a math teacher being cornered by a hyper-intense student strung out on caffeine who insists that numbers are just an *illusion*, man!

Scientists do not consistently reopen the basic methodology of the scientific method; economists are not continually overturning the essentials of their own profession – that human desires are limitless, but all resources are limited – and doctors do not continually debate the value of the Hippocratic Oath.

Surely, we can say, some basic aspects of human life can be accepted as given, so that we can have a firm foundation to build our edifices of thought upon. There are certain kinds of philosophers who will continually re-open the question of metaphysics and epistemology, and demand to know how we know that we are not living in the dream of an existential demon, and that everything is a managed illusion, and that we may in fact be a brain in a tank in a form of Matrix! These sorts of "thinkers" do bring up intellectually stimulating questions, to be sure, but there are very few of us who do not inevitably shrug our shoulders after failing to penetrate this veil of ignorance, and shake off the burden of these unanswerable questions, certain that we still have a life to live in the real world, and that to sit and forever ponder these unanswerable questions would be to sink into a form of hyper-intellectual coma.

Finally, let us suppose that it would be a good thing to get rid of the government – well, it might also be nice if we could fly, breathe underwater and sneeze gold! An essential component of rational prioritization is to recognize and separate the possible from the impossible. It may indeed be the case that we live in the dream of a demon, but so what? What possible difference could it make to our daily life if this were, or were not, the case? If it is utterly impossible to get rid of the government – at least in our own lifetime – then isn't it just a kind of narcissistic self-indulgence to continue to play around with the idea as if it ever could be implemented? We could also theorize that spending a solid week in zero gravity could be an excellent cure for lung cancer, but that would scarcely help the people suffering in our own lifetime. Surely, those of us with the intellectual abilities to traverse such endless abstractions should use our abilities for a more tangible and immediate good, rather than perform the intellectual equivalent of inventing the inner workings of Klingon biology.

We certainly do have the right to be skeptical about those who take their intellectual powers and run off in hot pursuit of the impossible – what could possibly be their motivation? Why would anyone want to get involved in a series of ideas that can never be achieved, that are alienating and frustrating to discuss, that eject these thinkers from anywhere close to the mainstream of social thought – and which create endless awkward silences at dinner parties, sweaty-palmed avoidances in one's early dating life, endless impossibilities in educational environments, teeth-grinding frustration when reading the newspaper or watching a movie, a reputation for eccentric and strangely intense thinking patterns, habitual eye-rolling from friends, a suspicious intellectual monomania that people kind of have to steer around if they wish to avoid "setting you off" – and, last but not least, some fairly endless challenges when it comes to raising your children, and filling them full of ideas that will doubtless set them approximately one solar system's league away from their peers.

It seems like an entirely generous estimate to imagine that more than one in 100 people will ever be interested in learning more about anarchism – and perhaps one out of a thousand will avidly pursue the course of thought and become full-fledged anarchists. What are the odds that these incredibly rare creatures will just happen to be scattered around the budding anarchist's social, familial and educational spheres?

Statistically, anarchism is a surefire recipe for social and familial isolation. After the virus of anarchism infects you, the possibility of infecting others remains very low – thus, you must either retreat to some sort of mental cave, or live a psychologically-perilous form of double life, biting your tongue and averting your eyes whenever the topic of politics, economics or the State comes up.

Given all these dire social consequences – combined with the fact that anarchism will never be implemented in our lifetime – how can we possibly understand the pursuit and acceptance of these wild ideas as anything other than a kind of intellectual shell around a hyper-tender personality, designed to alienate, frustrate and drive people away, perhaps as a result of a tortuous history of parental rejection?

Other than a strange and perverse kind of emotional masochism, what could conceivably motivate someone to take such a mad, vain, futile and unachievable intellectual course?

Surely, even if anarchism is sane, anarchists are not.

It is certainly true that there are many strange people in this world who believe many strange things – and that some of those strange people believe in anarchism. Stalin was both an evil sociopath and an atheist; Hitler was a murderous racist who also knew how to tie his shoes – this does not tell us anything about atheists or people who know how to tie their shoes as a whole.

A Merely Personal Confession…

I can say for myself – and I only mean this for myself – that although the truth often does press down like the weight of a cathedral on my sometimes-sloping shoulders, and though it does lower a dark and rippled glass between myself and the companions and family of my youth, and though it startles and scatters shocked glances in the faces of those around me, and although it renders the present unstable and the future uncertain – even with all that the truth demands and imposes upon me, I would not let you tear it from my heart with any power at your command.

The truth was not something that I set out to pursue. I dabbled in ideas when I was a child, just as I dabbled in playing certain instruments and painting in watercolor – never once dreaming that it would be anything other than a mildly diverting hobby. Looking back on it now, many decades later, it reminds me of one of those horror stories which depicts the disastrous consequences that result from "delving too deep" into the earth. Some sort of unholy beast arises from the depths and lays waste to the surface world – a beast that has lain dormant for hundreds or thousands of years is suddenly disturbed, and awakes with a sky-splitting roar, and a savage and unquenchable hunger for destruction.

During that shock of initial eruption, when the ideas that we started out merely playing with suddenly seem to take on a life of their own, like the escalating spells of Mickey Mouse, we do recoil in horror and leap back as if laser-scoped by a trigger-happy sniper, but we quickly learn the lesson of all horror stories, which is that the monsters are never outside our head.

The truth is an angry, demanding and liberating coach, who drags us kicking and screaming up a sharp and broken mountainside, and then sets us down gently to marvel in breathless wonder at the most beautiful view that can ever be conceived. As our complaints roll emptily down to disappear into the fogs of our past, in a bare ripple of white smoke, our eyes stream with tears in mute gratitude at what we have been able to behold.

Such happy and driven fools often look quite mad to those around them. The truth is a drug that renders the motives of those who pursue it incomprehensible and strangely disturbing to everyone else. The ferocity of truth's beauty is utterly beyond addictive; there is a passion and almost desperation to regain and reenter the perfection of consistent reason and the beauty of the clicking matchup between thought and observation. It keeps us awake even when we are exhausted; it strikes us with fits of passion even when we must be both silent and still; it obscures mere faces and opens up real minds; it peels away all the petty shallowness of the world and reveals all the glories and horrors of true depth.

And that makes it all worth it. The pursuit of truth only seems like masochism to those who have not tasted its joys. If your personal pleasures tend to center around social acceptance, then you unconsciously know – or perhaps consciously – that the pursuit of philosophical truth and wisdom will strip away that which gives you the most happiness in the moment. In a very real sense, you are huddling at the oasis of small-minded social pleasures, and cannot see beyond the desert that surrounds you, to a wider and greater world.

Unfortunately, there are very few philosophers who will help you to let go of this illusion. Most philosophers will talk endlessly about the beauty of the world beyond the desert, but will not confidently lead people away from the oasis they cling to. "You really should come with me," they say, "because this oasis is pretty bad, you know, and there is this wonderful world beyond the desert that we should all go to!" And they tug at everyone's trousers and endlessly cajole everyone to start marching across the desert to this wonderful new world – which baffles and irritates everyone in sight.

"If this new world is so wonderful, and it is supposed to set you so free, then why does the sum total of your freedom appear to be nothing more than your endless insistence that we all follow you out into the desert? If our world is actually so small, petty and unsatisfying, then why do you spend your time here, rather than in this new world that gives you such endless pleasure and freedom? Because we must tell you directly that it appears to us that you are also afraid of this desert, and you do not wish to cross it alone, and so you are desperate to find people who will come with you, because you do not in fact believe in this wonderful new world of happiness and freedom. If you had cancer, and you had discovered a cure for it, you would not refrain from taking that cure until you had convinced everyone else with cancer to take it. Rather, you would take the cure, and document everything with as much detail as possible, so that you could better make the case to others that they should take your cure. But, this is not what you are doing. You say that you have a cure for unhappiness called "wisdom," but this "cure" seems to require that everyone else take it at the same time. You do not appear to be willing to lead by example, but instead seem to be enslaved by a compulsive need to get everyone else to take this red pill at the same time that you do. Your pursuit of wisdom has clearly not given you the freedom, happiness and peace of mind that you claim it does – that you portray as a benefit in order to sell it to others. The world is full of people who will try to sell you 'cures' that they will not take themselves, and there is no good reason to believe that your claim that philosophical wisdom leads to happiness is any different!"

This basic paradox enslaves everyone at the oasis. The anarchist or philosopher, it turns out, is only tortured by his vision of the world beyond the desert – and in fact is only reinforcing everyone's belief in the necessity of social conformity for the achievement and maintenance of happiness. In this way, the philosopher is actually turning everyone *against* the pursuit of wisdom, for the sake of his own social anxieties. He is actually portraying philosophy as that which tortures you with a vision that you cannot achieve, but that you must continually harass others to pursue.

Finally, since the philosopher seems utterly unable to even *perceive* this basic paradox – let alone solve it – how much credibility are those around him going to grant his ability to perceive, pursue and capture the truth? If I claim to be a wonderful mathematician, and go on and on about the glories of exploring numbers, but all that anyone ever sees is my continual frustration at the fact that no one else seems to be very interested in math – and my complete inability to balance my checkbook, or even notice that it doesn't add up – then will I not be perceived as a kind of arrant fool, motivated by heaven knows what?

The "desert" metaphor is somewhat limited, since when we leave the oasis and cross the desert, we pass completely out of view. However, when we pursue the truth from our love of truth, and shrug off those who do not wish to join us, we do arise as a beacon in our social world, a sort of lighthouse that can help guide the few who are capable of being seized by such a love of truth that they are willing to give up the immediate creature and social comforts of living in a world of lies.

Those of us who cross the desert first can be deemed the most courageous in a way, but I must confess that in fact my journey felt less like a fish who braves leaving the water for the shore than a fish that is caught by the hook of philosophy and yanked unceremoniously from the depths. The future pulled me forward – against my will at times – and it was with great regret that I left almost everyone behind. I was not convinced of the glories of the world beyond the desert, but rather feared that the desert would go on forever, and that actually I might go mad. Fortunately to say the least, this did not happen, and I did discover the world beyond the desert, and all the beauties and truths that it contains.

By the time that my particular journey had slowed to at least a walking pace, I felt very little desire to go back to the oasis and try and get my former companions to join me in this new world. Once we have made the wrenching transition from ignorance to wisdom, we genuinely understand and appreciate the difficulty of the process, and would no more imagine dragging our former companions across this desert than we would choose a random person on the street to join us in an ascent of Everest.

At the end of my last book, I talked about a small village inhabited by those of us who have made it across this desert. I believe that it is our job, if we choose it, to make this little village as hospitable and inviting as possible for those few hardy, thirsty souls that we can see struggling out of the shimmering heat of the sand dunes. Creating a place where truth is welcome is the first goal for us pioneers. We know that we cannot return to the half life that we had before; we know that it would be selfish to continue on and on in the path of wisdom without creating some markers and resting places for those who are following us; and we know that the incredible advances in communication technology have for the first time in history allowed the path across the desert to be mapped and visible.

Never before has it been so relatively inviting to pursue the path of truth and wisdom. The destination is no longer the Socratic cup of hemlock, or Nietzsche's madness, or Rand's later cultishness, or the dry death of academic conformity – but rather a gathering place – a forum, I would say – where we can exchange ideas and experiences, and support each other, and learn how to best defend ourselves against those who would do us harm, and build our new homes – virtual though they may be for many – in the company of others, rather than alone, which has so often been the case in the past.

As we make our new homes more comfortable and inviting, we will in fact begin to draw more and more people across the desert, because they will see that there is a destination that can be achieved, and they will get more than a glimpse of the life that can be lived beyond lies. No sailor can navigate by the stars if the night is overcast – or if only one star is visible. As more and more stars wink into view, the navigation becomes easier and easier.

If you are tempted to pursue the freedom of truth and wisdom – or, to be more accurate, if the skyhook of truth and wisdom snatches you into some unsuspected stratosphere – then the choice has to some degree been made for you. To hang suspended between the worlds of conformity and wisdom is to live in a kind of null zone, where you gain neither the satisfactions of conformity nor the joys of wisdom.

It can be truly hard to leave those behind who cannot or will not join you on this journey, and the only consolation that I have been able to offer myself – and which I offer to you now – is that there could be nothing better to do with our lives than to create a world where we do not have to choose between wisdom and companions, between virtue and society – where a unity with truth will not mean a disunity with those around us.

A Few Principles…

Rather than repeat them every time I make an argument, I wanted to put a few principles out up front, before we begin.

First and foremost, although I am an anarchist, I am not a utopian. There is no social system which will utterly eliminate evil. In a stateless society, there will still be rape, theft, murder and abuse. To be fair, just and reasonable, we must compare a stateless society not to some standard of otherworldly perfection, but rather to the world as it already is. The moral argument for a stateless society includes the reality that it will eliminate a large amount of institutionalized violence and abuse, not that it will result in a perfectly peaceful world, which of course is impossible. Anarchy can be viewed as a cure for cancer and heart disease, not a prescription for endlessly perfect health. It would be unreasonable to oppose a cure for cancer because such a cure did not eliminate all other possible diseases – in the same way, we cannot reasonably oppose a stateless society because some people are bad, and a free society will not make them good.

Secondly, I am not proposing any Manichaean view of human nature in this book. I do not believe that human beings are either innately good, or innately evil. I take a very conservative and majority view, which is that human beings respond to incentives, which also happens to be the basis for the discipline of economics. Human beings are not innately corrupt, but they will inevitably be corrupted by power. Most people will respond to situations and circumstances in a way that maximizes their advantage, not explicitly at the expense of others, though that can happen of course, but we are biological as well as moral beings, and there are very few people who will sacrifice the safety and security of their family in order to follow some abstract moral principle. When human beings are forced to choose between virtue and necessity, they will in general choose necessity, and will then rework their definition of virtue to justify their own actions.

That having been said, it seems very clear that human beings are driven to a very large and deep degree by *virtue*. A man can almost never be convinced to do what he defines as evil – but if that evil can be redefined as a good, men will almost inevitably praise or perform it. Very few men would agree to murder for payment – but very few men will condemn soldiers as murderers.

Very few people would openly say that they oppose rape, but support the rapists – however, when the same moral equation is redefined as a good, just about everyone says that they oppose the war, but support the troops.

This is one of the lessons that I explicitly take from our existing ruling class, which is that the power of propaganda to redefine evil as good is a fundamental mechanism for controlling people and making them do what you want. Before any government can truly expand, it first needs to take control of the money supply, in order to bribe citizens, and the educational system, in order to indoctrinate children. A large percentage of the army's communications budget is dedicated to propaganda, and I assume that these people know more than a little about how to best spend money to control the minds of others.

Thus, I do understand that the reason that the debate about a stateless society is so volatile and aggressive is because anarchists are fundamentally attempting to reclaim the definition of virtue in society – and since society as a collective is largely defined by generally-accepted definitions of virtue, the anarchist approach to ethics is an attempt to fundamentally rewrite society as a whole.

Prior attempts to do this have almost always resulted in disaster, because they have always relied on gaining control of the government and using its power to impose some new version of ethics on a disarmed citizenry. The anarchist approach is particularly unsettling because we say that initiating violence to solve social problems is a great evil – perhaps the greatest evil – and so we steadfastly reject and refuse political solutions.

In the current world of governments, not only is political violence used to solve ethical problems, but also the use of such violence is itself considered virtuous and wise. Thus anarchists are entirely above the existing debate, because we are not trying to grab the gun and point it in the direction that we approve of, but rather are pointing out that violence cannot be used to achieve a positive good within society. Thus not only are existing solutions immoral, but the entire methodology for solving problems is based on a moral evil – the initiation of the use of force.

This is a fundamental rewrite of society, and people are right to be concerned and skeptical about the anarchist approach. It is the most fundamental transition that can be imagined – it is the difference between asking how slaves can be treated better, and stating that slavery is an irredeemable moral evil. It is the difference between asking what transgressions children should be beaten for, and stating that beating children is always and forever immoral.

USING THE PAST TO JUSTIFY THE FUTURE...

An objection to anarchism that I hear fairly often is that human beings are not so constituted as to be able to productively and intelligently rule themselves.

This objection rests on such a fundamental error that it is worth dealing with up front, since it will show up time and again in the upcoming arguments for anarchism.

We can all understand that it would be completely irrational to say that slaves cannot be freed, because they lack initiative and education. We all perfectly understand that slaves are barred from education, and punished for taking initiative. It is like saying that a totalitarian economy cannot be privatized because all of the workers are lazy – it is clear that this "laziness" actually arises out of a totalitarian economy, rather than any innate habits of the workers. Nutritionists might as well say that fat people cannot lose weight, because they are fat. The entire purpose of an expert is to help undo the habits that ignorance and a lack of opportunity has bred, and substitute more rational and positive behaviors in their place.

It is certainly true that people who come out of a statist educational system tend to be functionally retarded in many ways – they do not understand law, they do not understand politics, they do not understand economics, they do not understand philosophy, they have very likely never taken a course in logic – or even been offered one – they do not understand the scientific method, and they fundamentally do not know how to think or debate from first principles.

These are just the natural and disgusting results of the existing system – to say that men cannot be free because they lack the habits that freedom would have inculcated is a completely circular argument – it is like saying that newborn chicks of geese that have had their wings clipped can never fly, or that the daughter of a Chinese woman who suffered through foot binding will be born with bound feet.

Rejecting the virtues of the future for the sake of the evils of the past creates a closed-loop system that we can never escape. When anarchism comes to pass, there will doubtless be challenging and wrenching transitions for many people – but so what? This is actually an argument *for* anarchism, rather than against it. The harder that it is to transition out of a violent statist society, the more it is necessary to do so, and to prevent it from ever reemerging again. We do not say that heroin is less dangerous because it is so hard to quit, or so addictive – this is a central reason why heroin should not be taken in the first place! Constantly increasing our dosage of heroin because it is hard to quit would scarcely be a rational response to the problem of deadly addiction. The harder it is to quit, the more we should try to quit it, and the more we should strive to avoid re-addiction.

You are not the only kind person on the planet...

Another point that I would like to make up front is that there always seems to be a strange disconnect or isolation in people's concerns about the helpless and dependent in society.

For instance, whenever I talk about getting rid of public schools, the response inevitably comes back – automatically, it would seem, just like any other good propaganda – that it would be terrible, because poor children would not be educated.

There is a strange kind of unthinking narcissism in this response, which always irritates me, much though I understand it. First of all, it is rather insulting to be told that you are trying to design a system which would deny education to poor children. To be placed into the general category of "yuppie capitalist scum" is never particularly ennobling.

A person will raise this objection with an absolutely straight face, as if he is the *only person in the world* who cares about the education of poor children. I know that this is the result of pure indoctrination, because it is so illogical.

If we accept the premise that *very few people* care about the education of the poor, then we should be utterly opposed to majority-rule democracy, for the obvious reason that if only a tiny minority of people care about the education of the poor, then there will never be enough of them to influence a democracy, and thus the poor will never be educated.

However, those who approve of democracy and accept that democracy will provide the poor with education inevitably accept that a significant majority of people care enough about the poor to agitate for a political solution, and pay the taxes that fund public education.

Thus, any democrat who cares about the poor automatically accepts the reality that a significant majority of people are both willing and able to help and fund the education of the poor.

If people are willing to agitate for and pay the taxes to support a State-run solution to the problem of education, then the State solution is a mere *reflection* of their desires and willingness to sacrifice their own self-interest for the sake of educating the poor.

If I pay for a cure for an ailment that I have, and I find out that that cure actually makes me worse, do I give up on trying to find a cure? Of course not. It was my *desire* to find a cure that drove me to the false solution in the first place – when I accept that that solution is false, I am then free to pursue another solution. (In fact, until I accept that my first "cure" actually makes me worse, I will continue to waste my time and resources.)

The democratic "solution" to the problem of educating the poor is the existence of public schools – if we get rid of that solution, then the majority's desire to help educate the poor will simply take on another form – and a far more effective form, that much is guaranteed.

"Ah," say the democrats, "but without being forced to pay for public schools, no one will surrender the money to voluntarily fund the education of poor children."

Well, this is only an admission that democracy is a complete and total lie – that public schools do *not* represent the will of the majority, but rather the whims of a violent minority. Thus votes do not matter at all, and are not counted, and do not influence public policy in the least, and thus we should get rid of this ridiculous overhead of democracy and get right back to a good old Platonic system of minority dictatorship.

This proposal, of course, is greeted with outright horror, and protestations that democracy must be kept because it is the best system, because public policy *does* reflect the will of the majority.

In which case we need have no fear that the poor will not be educated in a free society, since the majority of people very much want that to happen anyway.

Exactly the same argument applies to a large number of other statist "solutions" to existing problems, such as:

* Old-age pensions;
* Unemployment insurance;
* Health care for the impoverished;
* Welfare, etc.

If these State programs represent the desires and will of the majority, then removing the government will not remove the reality of this kind of charity, since government policies reflect the majority's existing desire to help these people.

If these programs do *not* represent the desires and will of the majority, then democracy is a complete lie, and we should stop interfering with our leader's universal benevolence with our distracting and wasteful "voting."

We will get into this in more detail as we go forward, but I wanted to put the argument out up front, just to address the ridiculous objection that removing a democratic State also removes the benevolence that drives its policies.

A fundamental anarchic argument is that a democratic State uses the genuine benevolence of the majority to expand its own power, and exacerbates poverty, ignorance and sickness in order to justify and continue the expansion of that power.

This is not the first time that the benevolence of good people has been used to control them.

We only need to think of the example of organized religion to understand that…

One final point, and then we shall begin really rolling up our sleeves and having some fun figuring out how a free society can truly work.

Although the ideas of anarchy can be alarming, it is important to remember that anarchy is not an untried and untested system. As I talked about in my last book, anarchy is the foundation of how we organize our own personal lives, and it is also the root of how the government manages to survive, at least for as long as it does, despite its corrupt and evil nature.

Prior approaches to re-writing social ethics failed because they did not evolve out of what works in our personal lives. We fully accept that theories of physics cannot contradict that which is directly observable within our own lives; that which describes a falling planet cannot contradict our direct perception of a falling brick.

Indeed, since we would so strenuously resist the incursion of State power into our own personal and practical "anarchy," it can be easier to understand how *statism* is a violent and artificial solution, not anarchy.

If we look at something like communism, we can see that it represented a radical reversal of what actually works in our own personal lives. We retain and trade property constantly in our own lives. Stripping us of the right to own and trade property is an entirely artificial "oppositional solution," which is why it had to be imposed through endless violence, murder and imprisonment.

In the same way, when we look at something like religion, we can see that it represents a radical reversal of what we actually believe to be true in our own personal lives. Children do not need threats, bribes and propaganda to believe that the sun will rise tomorrow, that gravity works and concrete is hard on the knees. They do not need to be bullied in order to learn language, or grow physically and mentally, or ask endless questions and explore their environment.

However, to believe that some ancient and fantastical Jewish zombie died for their "sins," and that they are trailed and judged by an omnipresent and invisible ghost, and that they need to eat and drink symbolic flesh and blood to commune with some universal and incorporeal mind – well, that takes an enormous amount of propaganda, bribery and bullying. Religion is an entirely artificial "oppositional solution" to the question of existence and ethics. It must be repetitively and aggressively inflicted on children, because it scarcely comes naturally to them at all.

Anarchy, however, does not fall into this category.

For instance, when you face a problem at work, I can't imagine that you ever sit your team down and say:

"I've come up with the perfect solution to our problem – what we're going to do, see, is pick two of us, give them guns, and then those two are going to force the rest of us to do whatever they want for the next few years, and then we are going to perhaps pick two *other* people who will get those guns, and then *they'll* be able to force us to do whatever they want us to do for the next few years, and then we'll start all over again…"

I have yet to see a business book with anything close to the title of: "Creating A Violent Internal Monopoly To Solve Your Customer Service Woes!"

In the same way, if you face problems in your relationship, you may go to a marriage counselor, but I have never heard of any couple going to the Mafia, and saying: "We can't quite agree on how we should be spending our money, so we're going to buy you guys a bunch of guns and bombs, and we want you to tell us what to do, and if we disobey your orders, we want you to kidnap us and throw us in some dank and horrible cell, where we can only hope to be raped by other people!"

If you are looking for a job, I do not imagine that you will kidnap someone and force him to hire you. If you want a girlfriend, or a boyfriend, I cannot believe that you will chloroform and kidnap someone you are attracted to, like the protagonist in John Fowles's "The Collector."

If you are having trouble parenting, it does not seem at all likely that you will hire someone to kidnap you if you parent in a way that he disagrees with for some reason.

This list can of course go on and on, but the basic reality is that we never look for statist solutions to problems that we face in our own lives. We never create a localized monopoly, arm it and give it the right to take half our income at gunpoint, and then force us to obey its whims.

STATISM AND ISOLATION

There is something about statism, some aspect of it, which profoundly isolates us from our fellow citizens. We turn from animated problem-solvers to mindless defenders of the status quo. As an example, I offer up the inevitable response I receive when I provide an anarchic solution to an existing State function. When I say that theoretical entities called Dispute Resolution Organizations (DROs) could enforce contracts and protect property, the immediate response is that these DROs will inevitably evolve into a single monopoly that will end up recreating the State that they were supposed to replace.

Or, when I talk about private roads, I inevitably hear the argument that someone could just build a road in a ring around your land and charge you a million dollars every time you wanted to cross it.

Or, when I talk about private defense agencies that can be used to protect a geographical region from invasion, I am promptly informed that those private agencies will simply turn their guns on their subscribers, take them over, and create a new State.

Or, when I discuss the power of economic ostracism as a tool for maintaining order and conformity to basic social and economic rules, I am immediately told that people will be "marked for exclusion" unless they pay hefty bribes to whatever agencies control such information.

It is the same story, over and over – an anarchic solution is provided, and an immediate "disaster scenario" is put forward without thought, without reflection, and without curiosity.

Of course, I am not bothered by the fact that people are critical of a new and volatile theory – I think that is an essential process for any new idea.

What *does* concern me is the fundamental lack of *reciprocity* in the minds of the people who thoughtlessly reject creative solutions to trenchant problems.

I don't mean reciprocity with regards to me – though that is surely lacking as well – but rather with regards to any form of authority or influence in general.

For instance, if people in a geographical region want to contract with an agency or group of agencies for the sake of collective defense, what is the greatest fear that will be first and foremost in their minds?

Naturally, it will be that some defense agency will take their money, buy a bunch of weapons, and promptly enslave them.

How does a free society solve this problem? Well, if there is a market need or demand for collective defense, a number of firms will vie for the business, since it will be so lucrative in the long term. The economic efficiency of having a majority of subscribers would drive the price of such defense down – however, the more people that you enroll in such a contract, the greater everyone's fear will be that this defense agency will attempt to become a government of some kind.

Thus no entrepreneur will be able to sell this service in the most economically efficient manner *if he does not directly and credibly address the fear that he will attempt to create a new government.*

We are so used to being on the one-sided receiving end of dictatorial edicts from those in power – whether they are parents, teachers, or government officials, that the very *idea* that someone is going to have to woo our trust is almost incomprehensible. "If I am afraid of something that someone wants to sell me, then it is up to that person to calm my fears if he wants my business" – this is so far from our existing ways of dealing with statist authority that we might as well be inventing a new planet.

It is so important to understand that when we are talking about a free society – and I will tell you later how this habit is so essential for your happiness even if anarchism *never* comes to pass – we are essentially talking about *two sides* of a negotiation table.

When it comes to government as it is – and all that government ever could be – we are never really talking about two sides of the table. You get a letter in the mail informing you that your property taxes are going to increase 5% – there is no negotiation;

no one offers you an alternative; your opinion is not consulted beforehand, and your approval is not required afterwards, because if you do not pay the increased tax, you will, after a fairly lengthy sequence of letters and phone calls, end up without a house.

It is certainly true that your local cable company may also send you a notice that they're going to increase their charges by 5%, but that is *still* a negotiation! You can switch to satellite, or give up on cable and rent DVDs of movies or television shows, or reduce some of the extra features that you have, or just decide to get rid of your television and read and talk instead.

None of these options are available with the government – with the government, you either pay them, give up your house, go to jail, or move to some other country, where the exact same process will start all over again.

Can you imagine getting *this* letter from your cable company?

Dear Valued Customer:

Your cable bill is now increasing 5% per month. You cannot cancel your cable. Ever. You cannot reduce your bill in any way. If you turn off your cable, your bill will remain exactly the same. If you rip your cable out of the wall, your bill will remain exactly the same, with the exception that we will charge you for the damage. Your children will be unable to cancel your cable contract.

Also, please note that we will be reducing our delivery of channels by approximately 1 every month. As we deliver fewer channels, you can anticipate that your bill will sharply increase.

If you do not pay your bill on time, the ownership of your house will revert to us, and we will lock you in an undisclosed location, where you will be forced to do tech support, and where we will be unable to protect you from assault and rape.

If you attempt to defend yourself when we come to take your house, we are fully authorized to gun you down.

Sincerely,

The Statist Cable Company

We would consider this kind of letter to be utterly criminal – and we would be outraged at the dictatorial one-sidedness of the letter, as well as the threats of violence it contained.

Unfortunately, this is exactly the kind of communication that we get from our governments all the time – and in many ways, it is not unrelated to the kind of non-negotiated dictums that we received from our teachers when we were children.

Thus, when a philosopher of anarchy proposes private solutions to public services, we automatically and almost unconsciously feel that we are back on the receiving end of one-sided and dictatorial commandments, and fear this multiplicity of small "quasi-governments," and imagine that instead of receiving a few such ugly letters a year, we shall get perhaps dozens per month.

However, if you do not understand that anarchism is always and forever a *two-sided negotiation*, then you will remain forever untempted by its rational and empirical pleasures, and continue to confuse coercion with voluntarism, which is about the most fundamental error that can be made in moral understanding.

If you feel the need for collective defense, but you are afraid that whoever you contract with for such defense will end up ruling over you, you can just sit back, put your feet up on the desk, clasp your hands behind your head, and just see who comes along with an offer that satisfies you.

Once you grasp this fundamental shift in thinking – in understanding – then you can "flip over" to the other side of the table and use your real creative mojo to start solving the problem.

In this way, you can ask yourself, "If I really wanted to sell collective defense services to a group, how could I best address and alleviate their fears that I would turn into some kind of local dictator?"

What do you think? If you could personally make $10 million a year by solving this problem, what would you come up with? How would you address and alleviate people's fears that you would take their money, go buy an army, and rule over them?

There are as many creative and productive answers as there are people interested in the problem – here's one that occurs to me, just off the top of my head…

I would deposit $5 million in a third-party bank account, and offer it as free payment to anyone who could prove that I was not fulfilling my contract with my customers to the letter. I would publish my accounts and inventory as widely as possible, and give free access to anyone who wanted to come by and inspect my business and its holdings.

In this way, people could rest assured that I was not amassing some secret army of black helicopters and men in robot suits.

"Ah," you may say, "but what if no one wanted to come forward and perform these kinds of inspections?"

Again, that is easy to solve. I would just pay an organization $1 million a year to audit my business – and promise them that if they *ever* found me accumulating any kind of secret army or weaponry, then I would then pay them the $5 million in the third party bank account. In this way, external audits would be certain to be performed, and those auditors would have every incentive to turn over every filing cabinet in search of a miniature robot army.

"Ah," you may say, "but what if you were secretly paying this auditing organization $2 million a year to only *pretend* to audit your business?"

Well, here we are starting to get into some very strange economic territory, which would be utterly unsustainable in a free market, because my company would then be out $5 million up front, be paying $1 million for an auditing company, and then a further $2 million to produce fake audits – such a company would never be able to offer competitive rates relative to a company that operated on the up and up.

But even if this were possible, it would still be an easy problem to solve, by simply paying five companies to perform audits if necessary – paying $5 million a year out of a profit of $10 million a year still leaves you $5 million ahead!

"Ah, but what if..?"

We all know that this game can go on for forever and a day – the mindset that I strongly urge you to try and get yourself into, however, is that *you do not have to contract with anyone who is not willing to satisfy your desires!*

Relative Risk

What happens if no entrepreneur is able to offer you a deal that successfully calms your fears?

Why, then you do not have to take any deal at all.

"Ah," you may then say, "but then I am leaving myself open to the risk of foreign invasion!"

Well, that is very true, but clearly, if you reject all offers from entrepreneurs who want to protect you, because you feel that their protection carries too much risk, then clearly you prefer the risk of invasion to the risk of protection.

With that in mind, you may well choose one entrepreneur's scheme – not because it is risk-free, but rather because it is *less* risky than the risk of invasion.

If you wish to be presented with a risk-*free* choice, then unfortunately you wish to be presented with a different kind of universe than the one we inhabit, since risk is an inevitable and natural part of life.

With that in mind, let us turn to one of the first great objections to the idea of a stateless society, which is collective defense, to provide an example of the methodologies we will use in this book.

COLLECTIVE DEFENSE: AN EXAMPLE OF METHODOLOGY

Ideally, invasions should be prevented rather than repelled, just as illnesses should be prevented rather than cured.

The strongest conceivable case for anarchism is that a stateless society would by its very nature *prevent* invasion, rather than merely possess the ability to violently repel it.

So first, before we figure out how to repel an invasion, let us look at what an invasion is actually designed to achieve.

WHY INVADE?

Let us imagine a land where there are two farms, owned by Bob and Jim respectively. Bob is a rapacious and nasty fellow, who wishes to expand his farm and make more money.

To the east of Bob is Jim's farm, which is tidy, efficient, and productive, with a wide variety of cows and chickens and neatly-planted fields.

To the west of Bob is an untamed wilderness full of bears and wolves and coyotes and mosquitoes and swamps and all other sorts of unpleasant and dangerous things.

From the standpoint of mere practical considerations, how can Bob most efficiently expand his farm and increase his income?

Surely it would be to invest in a few guns, head east, and take over Jim's farm. For a very small investment, Bob ends up with a functioning and productive farm, ready to provide him with milk, eggs and crops.

On the other hand, Bob could choose to go west, into the untamed wilderness, and try to cull a number of dangerous predators, drain the swamps, hack down and uproot all the embedded trees and bushes. After a year or two of backbreaking labor, he may have carved out a few additional acres for himself – an investment that would scarcely seem worth it.

If Bob wants to expand, and cares little about ethics, he will "invade" Jim's farm and take it over, because he will be taking command of an already-existing system of exploitation and production.

Thus, we can see that the act of invading a neighboring territory is primarily motivated by the desire to take over an existing productive system. If that productive system is not in place, then the motivation for invasion evaporates. A car thief will never "steal" a rusted old jalopy that is sitting up on bricks in an abandoned lot, but rather will attempt to steal a car that is in good condition.

This analysis of the costs and benefits of invasion is essential to understanding how a stateless society actually works to prevent invasion, rather than merely repel it.

When one country invades another country, the primary goal is to take over the existing system of government, and thus collect the taxes from the existing citizens. In the same way that Bob will only invade Jim's farm in order to take over his domesticated animals, one government will only invade another country in order to take over the government of that country, and so become the new tax collector. If no tax collection system is in place, then there is no productive resource for the invading country to take over.

Furthermore, to take a silly example, we can easily understand that Bob will only invade Jim's farm if he knows that Jim's cows and chickens are not armed and dangerous. To adjust the metaphor a little closer to reality, imagine that Jim has a number of workers on his farm who are all ex-military, well-armed, and will fight to the death to protect that farm. The disincentive for invasion thus becomes considerably stronger.

In the same way, domestic governments generally keep their citizens relatively disarmed, in order to more effectively tax them, just as farmers clip the wings of their geese and chickens in order to more efficiently collect their eggs and meat.

Thus the cost-benefit analysis of invasion only comes out on the plus side if the benefits are clear and easy to attain – an existing tax collection system – and if the costs of invasion are relatively small – a largely disarmed citizenry.

In a very real sense, therefore, a stateless society *cannot* be invaded, because there is really nothing to invade. There are no government buildings to inhabit, no existing government to displace, no tax collection system in place to take over and profit from – and, furthermore, there is no clear certainty about the degree of armaments that each citizen possesses (don't worry, we will get into gun control later…).

An invading country can be very certain that, if it breaks through another government's military defenses, it will then not face any significant resistance from the existing citizenry. A statist society can be considered akin to an egg – if you break through the shell, there is no second line of defense inside. Invading governments are well aware of the existing laws against the proliferation of weapons in the country they are invading – thus they are guaranteed to be facing a virtually disarmed citizenry, as long as they can break through the military defenses.

INVADING ANARCHY

Let us imagine that France becomes a stateless society, but that Germany and Poland do not. Let us go with the cliché and imagine that Germany has a strong desire to expand militarily. The German leader then looks at a map, and tries to figure out whether he should go east into Poland, or west into France.

If he goes east into Poland, then he will, if he can break through the Polish military defenses, be able to feast upon the existing tax base, and face an almost completely disarmed citizenry. He will be able to use the existing Polish tax collectors and tax collection system to enrich his own government, because the Poles are already controlled and "domesticated," so to speak.

In other words, he only has one enemy to overcome and destroy, which is the Polish government's military. If he can overcome that single line of defense, he gains control over billions of dollars of existing tax revenues every single year – and a ready-made army and its equipment.

On the other hand, if he thinks of going west into France, he faces some daunting obstacles indeed.

There are no particular laws about the domestic ownership of weapons in a stateless society, so he has no idea whatsoever which citizens have which weapons, and he certainly cannot count on having a legally-disarmed citizenry to prey on after defeating a single army.

Secondly, let us say that his army rolls across the border into France – what is their objective? If France still had a government, then clearly his goal would be to take Paris, displace the existing government, and take over the existing tax collection system.

However, where is his army supposed to go once it crosses the border? There is no capital in a stateless society, no seat of government, no existing system of tax collection and citizen control, no centralized authority that can be seized and taken over. In the above example of the two farms and the wilderness, this is the equivalent not of Bob taking over Jim's farm, but rather of Bob heading into the wilderness and facing coyotes, bears, swamps and mosquitoes – there is no single enemy, no existing resources to take over, and nothing in particular to "seize."

But let us say that the German leadership is completely retarded, and decides to head west into France anyway – and let us also suppose, to make the case as strong as possible, that everyone in France has decided to forego any kind of collective self-defense.

What is the German army going to do in France? Are they going to go door to door, knocking on people's houses and demanding their silverware? Even if this were possible, and actually achieved, all that would happen is that the silverware would be shipped back to Germany, thus putting German silverware manufacturers out of business. When German manufacturers go out of business, they lay people off, thus destroying tax revenue for the German government.

The German army cannot reasonably ship French houses to Germany – perhaps they will seize French cars and French electronics and ship *them* to Germany instead.

And what is the German government supposed to do with thousands of French cars and iPods? Are they supposed to sell these objects to their own citizens at vastly reduced prices? I imagine that certain German citizens would be relatively happy with that, but again, all that would happen is that German manufacturers of cars and electronics would be put out of business, thus again sharply reducing the German government's tax income, resulting in a net loss.

Furthermore, by destroying domestic industries for the sake of a one-time transfer of French goods, the German government would be crippling its own future income, since domestic manufacturing represents a permanent source of tax revenue – this would be a perfect example of killing the goose that lays the golden egg.

Well, perhaps what the German government could do is seize French citizens and ship them to Germany as slave labor. What would be the result of that?

Unfortunately, this would not work either, at least not for long, because slave labor cannot be taxed, and slave labor would displace existing German labor, which is taxable. Thus again the German government would be permanently reducing its own income, which it would not do.

Another reason that Germany might invade another country would be to seize control of the wealth of the government – the ability to print money, and the ownership of a large amount of physical assets, such as buildings, cars, gold, manufacturing plants and so on.

However, nothing remains unowned in a stateless society, except that which has no value, or cannot be owned, such as air. There are no "public assets" to seize, and there are no state-owned printing presses which can be used to create currency, and thus transfer capital to Germany. There are no endless vaults of government gold to rob, no single aggregation of military assets to seize.

Furthermore, if we go up to a thief and say to him, "Do you want to rob a house?" what is his first question likely to be?

"Hell I don't know – what's in it?"

A thief will always want to know the benefits of robbing a house – he is fully aware of the risks and costs, of course, and must weigh them against the rewards. He will never scale up the outside of some public housing welfare tenement in order to snag an old television and a tape deck. The more knowledgeable he is of the value of a home's contents, the better he is able to assess the value of breaking into it.

The German leadership, when deciding which country to invade, will know down to almost the last dollar the tax revenues being collected by the Polish government, as well as the value of the public assets they will seize if they invade. The "payoff" can be very easily assessed.

On the other hand, if they look west, into the French stateless society, how will they know what they are actually going to get? There are no published figures for the net wealth of the society as a whole, there is no tax revenue to collect, and there are no public assets which can be easily valued ahead of time. There is no way to judge the cost effectiveness of the invasion.

Invading a statist society is like grabbing the cages of a large number of trapped chickens – you get all of the eggs in perpetuity. Invading a stateless society is like taking a sprint at a flock of seagulls – all they do is scatter, and you get nothing, except perhaps some crap on your forehead.

Thus it is completely impossible that the German leadership would think it a good idea to head west into France rather than east into Poland.

We could leave the case here, and be perfectly satisfied in our responses, but I am always willing to go the extra mile and accept the worst conceivable case.

Let us say that some mad German who was beaten with bagfuls of French textbooks when he was a child ends up running the government, and cares nothing at all about the costs and benefits of invading France, but rather just wishes to take it over in order to – I don't know, burn all the textbooks or something like that.

We will get into the nature and content of private agencies in the next chapter, but let us just say that there are a number of these private defense agencies that are paid to defend France against just such an invading madman.

Well, if I were setting up some sort of private military defense agency, the first thing I would do is try to figure out how I could most effectively protect my subscribers, for the least possible cost.

The first thing that I would note is that nuclear weapons have been the single most effective deterrent to invasion that has ever been invented. Not one single nuclear power has ever been invaded, or threatened with invasion – and so, in a very real sense, there is no bigger "bang for the buck" in terms of defense than a few well-placed nuclear weapons.

If we assume that a million subscribers are willing to pay for a few nuclear weapons as a deterrent to invasion, and that those nuclear weapons cost about $30 million to purchase and maintain every year, then we are talking about $30 a year per subscriber – or less than a dime a day.

The defense agencies only make money if an invasion does not occur, just as health insurance companies only make money when you are not sick, but rather well.

Thus the question that I would be most keen to answer if I were running a defense agency is: "How can I best prevent an invasion?"

Let us assume that the French stateless society is a beacon of liberation in a sea of aggressive and statist nations. The French defense agencies would work day and night to ensure that the costs of invasion were as high as possible, and the benefits as low as possible. Were I running one of these agencies, I would think of solutions along the lines of the following…

DEACTIVATED MONEY

If I were concerned that my subscribers might be robbed by an invading army, I would offer reduced rates to those willing to allow their electronic money to be secured so that it could not be spent without their own thumb print, or something like that. (Naturally, any system can be hacked, and people can be kidnapped along with their money, but the purpose here is not to prevent all possible workarounds, but rather to simply reduce the material benefits of invading France.)

Similarly, I might offer reduced defense rates to manufacturers that would be willing to allow a small GPS device to be installed in the guts of their machinery, so that if it was removed to another country, it would no longer work. This device could also be included in cars and other items of value, so that they would either have to be used in France, or they could not be used at all.

Given that the control of bridges is a primary military objective, in order to facilitate the movement of troops and vehicles, I would also encourage the installation of particular devices in domestic cars and trucks, which would automatically keep access to bridges open. Thus invading armies would find their access to these bridges much harder, which would again slow down the speed of their invasion.

Furthermore, if invasion seemed imminent, I would arm and train as many citizens as possible. Any invading army would face a quite different challenge in a stateless society. If Germany invades Poland, how many citizens would risk their lives fighting against just another government? Whether a Polish leader taxes you, or a German one, makes relatively little difference – which is why your average citizen does not care much about who runs the local Mafia. Citizens of a stateless society, however, would be resisting an attempt to inflict taxation and a government upon them, and so would be far more willing to fight the kind of endlessly-draining insurgencies that we see so often in the annals of occupation.

These are just a few admittedly off-the-cuff ideas, but it is relatively easy to see how the benefits of invading France could be significantly diminished or even eliminated, while the costs of invading France could be significantly increased or made prohibitive.

The objection could be raised that some lunatic group could simply detonate a nuclear bomb somewhere inside France, for some insane or nefarious motive – but that is not an argument against private defense agencies, and for a statist society, but rather quite the reverse.

The "nuclear madman" argument is not solved by the existence of a government, since no government can protect against this eventuality – however, a free society would be far less likely to be the target of such an attack, since it would have a defensive military policy only, and not an aggressive and interventionist foreign policy, and thus would be infinitely less likely to provoke such a mad and genocidal retaliation. Switzerland, for instance, faces no real danger of having airplanes flown into buildings.

It is my belief that over time, the need for these proactive and defensive strategies would diminish, since the only thing that would really ever be needed is a few nuclear weapons as a deterrent – and even the need for these would diminish over time, since either the world itself would become stateless, thus eliminating the danger of war, or the statist societies would continue to attack each other only, for the reasons mentioned above, and the need to continually defend a stateless society would diminish.

Finally, let's look at some of the illusions that we have about statist "protection" in history, as a demonstration of how we can critically evaluate an example of a statist function.

STATIST NATIONAL "DEFENSE": A CRITICAL EXAMPLE

Briefly put, "national defense" is the need for a government to protect citizens from aggression by other governments.

This is an interesting paradox, even beyond the obvious one of using a "government" to protect us from "governments." If you were able to run a magic survey throughout history, which government do you think people would be most frightened of and enslaved by? Would it be (a), their local State or Lord, or (b), some State or Lord in some other country? What about ancient Rome – would it be the local rulers, who forced young Romans into military service for 20 years or more, or the Carthaginians? What about England in the Middle Ages? Were the peasants more alarmed by the crushing taxation and strangling mobility restrictions imposed by their local Lord, or was the King of France their primary concern? Let us stop in Russia during the 18th century, and ask the serfs: "Are you more frightened of the Tsar's soldiers, or the German Kaiser?" Let us go to a US citizen of today, and demand to know: "Are you more frightened of foreign invaders taking over Washington, or of the fact that if you don't pay half your income in taxes, your own government will throw you in jail?"

Of course, we have to look at the Second World War, which has had more propaganda thrown at it than any other single conflict. Didn't the British government save the country from Germany? That is an interesting question. The British government got into WWI, helped impose the brutal Treaty of Versailles, then contributed to the boom-and-bust cycle of the 1920s, which destroyed the German middle class and aided Hitler's rise to power. During the 1930s, the British government supported the growing aggression of Hitler through subsidies, loans and mealy-mouthed appeasement. Then, when everything had failed, it threw the bodies of thousands of young men at the German air force in the Battle of Britain. Finally, it caused the deaths of hundreds of thousands more British citizens by defending Africa and invading France, rather than let Nazism collapse on its own – as it was bound to do, just as every tyranny has done throughout history. Can it really be said, then, that the British government protected its citizens throughout the first half of the 20th century? Millions killed, families shattered, the economy destroyed, half of Europe lost to Stalin, and China to Mao... Can we consider that a great success? I think not. Only States win wars – never citizens.

The fact of the matter is that we do not face threats to our lives and property from *foreign* governments, but rather from our own. The State will tell us that it must exist, at the very least, to protect us from foreign governments, but that is morally equivalent to the local Mafia don telling us that we have to pay him 50% of our income so that he can protect us from the Mafia in Paraguay. Are we given the choice to buy a gun and defend ourselves? Of course not. Who endangers us more – the local Mafia guy, or some guy in Paraguay we have never met that our local Mafia guy says just might want a piece of us? I know which chance *I* would take.

There is a tried-and-true method for resisting foreign occupation which does not require any government – which we can see being played out in our daily news. During the recent invasion, the US completely destroyed the Iraqi government, and now has total control over the people and infrastructure. And what is happening? They are being attacked and harried until they will just have to get out of the country – just as they had to do in Korea and Vietnam, and just as the USSR had to do in Afghanistan. The Iraqi insurgents do not have a government at all – any more than the Afghani fighters did in the 1980s.

Let's look at the Iraqi conflict in a slightly different light. America was attacked on 9/11 because the American government had troops in Saudi Arabia, and because it caused the deaths of hundreds of thousands of Iraqis through the Iraqi bombing campaign of the 1990s. Given that the US government provoked the attacks, how well were the innocent victims of 9/11 protected by their government? Even if we do not count the physical casualties of the war, given the massive national debt being run up to pay for the Iraq war, how well is the *property* of American citizens being protected? How much power would Bush have to wage war if he did not have the power to steal almost half the wealth of the entire country? The government does not need taxes in order to wage war; it wages war because it already *has* the power of taxation – and it uses the war to raise taxes, either on the current citizens through increases and inflation, or on future citizens through deficits.

This simple fact helps explain why there were almost no wars in Western Europe from the end of the Napoleonic Wars in 1815 to the start of World War One in 1914. This was largely because governments could not afford wars – but then they all got their very own Central Banks and were able to pave the bloody path to the Great War with printed money and deficit financing. World War One *resulted* from an increase in State power – and in turn swelled State power, and set the stage for the next war. Thus, the idea that we need to give governments the power to tax us in order to *protect* us is ludicrous – because it is taxation that gives governments the power to wage war.

For pacifist countries, this "war" may be a war on poverty, or illiteracy, or drugs, or for universal health care, or whatever. It does not matter. The moment a government takes the power – and moral "right" – to forcibly take money from citizens, the stage is set for the ever-growing power of the State.

The question then arises – how does a citizen keep his property and person safe? The first answer that I would give is another question, which is:

Which sector does more to protect you and your property – the public or the private?

Let's look at the security mechanisms the private sector has introduced in just the past few decades:

- ATMs/credit cards (less need to carry cash);
- Cell phones (can always call for help);
- Call display (virtually eliminates harassing phone calls);
- Sophisticated home security systems;
- ID tracking tags;

- Credit card numeric security;
- Pepper spray;
- GPS;
- Security cameras;
- Anti-shoplifting devices;
- Secure online transactions;
- And much more…

What has the public sector done? Well, they shoot harmless drug users and seize their property. They will shoot you too, if you don't pay the massive tax increases they demand. The police are virtually useless in property crimes – and many violent criminals are turned loose because the courts are too slow, or are put in "house arrest" because the prisons are too full of non-violent offenders.

So, who has most helped you secure your person and property over the past few decades? Your government, or your friendly local entrepreneurs? Those who have stepped in to protect you, or those who have doubled your taxes while letting criminals walk free? Have capitalist companies enraged foreigners to the point of terrorism? Of course not – the 9/11 terrorists attacked the World Trade Center (to protest the financing of the US government), the Pentagon, and the White House. They didn't go for a Ford motor plant or a Apple store – and why would they? No one kills for iPhones. They kill to protest military power, which rests on public financing.

In summation, then, it makes about as much sense to rely on governments for security as it does to rely on the Mafia for "protection." The Mafia is really just protecting you from itself, as are all governments. Any man who comes up to you and says: "I need to threaten your person and steal your property in order to protect your person and property," is obviously either deranged, or not particularly interested, to say the least, in protecting your person and property. As long as we keep falling for the same old lies, we will forever be robbed blind for the sake of our supposed property rights, and sent to wage war against internal or external "enemies" so that those in power can further pick the pockets of those we leave behind.

PART 2

Reasoning

• • •

INTRODUCTION: THE SIX QUESTIONS

WHEN CONSIDERING STATIST OBJECTIONS TO anarchic solutions, the six questions below are most useful.

1. **Does the government actually *solve* the problem in question?**

   People often say that government courts "solve" the problem of injustice. However, these courts can take many years to render a verdict – and cost the plaintiff and defendant hundreds of thousands of dollars or more. Government courts are also used to harass and intimidate, creating a "chilling effect" for unpopular opinions or groups. Thus I find it essential to question the embedded premises of statism:

   - Do State armies actually defend citizens?
   - Does State policing actually protect private property?
   - Does State welfare actually solve the problem of poverty?
   - Does the war on drugs actually solve the problem of addiction and crime?
   - Do State prisons actually rehabilitate prisoners and reduce crime?

   It can be very tempting to fall into the trap of thinking that the existing statist approach is actually a solution – but I try to avoid taking that for granted, since it is so rarely the case.

2. **Can the criticism of the anarchic solution be equally applied to the statist solution?**

   One of the most common objections to a stateless society is the fear that a political monopoly could somehow emerge from a free market of competing justice agencies. In other words, anarchism is rejected because it contains the mere *possibility* of political monopoly. However, if political monopoly is such a terrible evil, then a statist society – which is founded on just such a political monopoly – must be rejected even more firmly, just as we would always choose the mere *possibility* of cancer over actually *having* cancer.

3. **Is anarchy accepted as a core value in nonpolitical spheres?**

   In my last book, "Everyday Anarchy," I pointed out the numerous spheres in society where anarchy is both valued and defended, such as dating, career choices, education and so on. If anarchy is dismissed as "bad" overall, then it also must be "bad" in these other spheres as well. Unless the person criticizing anarchy is willing to advocate for a Ministry of Dating, the value of anarchy in certain spheres must at least be recognized. Thus anarchy cannot be rejected as an overall negative – and its admitted value and productivity must at least be accepted as *potentially* valuable in other spheres as well.

4. **Would the person advocating statism perform State functions himself?**

   Most of us recognize and accept the right to use violence in an extremity of self-defense. Those who support statism recognize that, in this realm, State police merely formalize a right that everyone already has, namely the right of self-defense. A policeman can use force to protect a citizen from being attacked, just as that citizen can use force himself. However, if someone argues that it is moral to use force to take money from people to pay for public schools, would he be willing to use this force *himself*? Would he be willing to go door to door with a gun to extract money for public schools? Would he be willing to extend this right to everyone in society? If not, then he has created two opposing ethical categories – the State police, to whom this use of violence is *moral* – and everyone else, to whom this use of violence is *immoral*. How can these opposing moral categories be justified?

5. **Can something be both voluntary and coercive at the same time?**

   Everyone recognizes that an act cannot be both "rape" and "lovemaking" simultaneously. Rape requires force, because the victim is unwilling; lovemaking does not. Because no action can be both voluntary and coercive at the same time, statists cannot appeal to the principle of "voluntarism" when defending the violence of the State. Statists cannot say that we "agree" to be taxed, and then say that taxation must be coercive. If we agree to taxation, the coercion is unnecessary – if we do not agree to taxation, then we are coerced against our will.

6. **Does political organization change human nature?**

If people care enough about the poor to vote for state welfare programs, then they will care enough about the poor to fund private charities. If people care enough about the uneducated to vote for state schools, they will care enough to donate to private schools. Removing the State does not fundamentally alter human nature. The benevolence and wisdom that democracy relies on will not be magically transformed into cold selfishness the moment that the State ends. Statism relies on maturity and benevolence on the part of the voters, the politicians, and government workers. If this maturity and benevolence is not present, the State is a mere brutal tyranny, and must be abolished. If the majority of people *are* mature and benevolent – as I believe – then the State is an unnecessary overhead, and far too prone to violent injustices to be allowed to continue. In other words, people cannot be called "virtuous" only when it serves the statist argument, and then "selfish" when it does not.

There are a number of other principles, which are more specific to particular circumstances, but the six described above will show up repeatedly.

We will now take a quick tour through an overview of anarchism, and sketch in broad strokes the beginnings of our solutions to the horrors of worldwide violence.

ANARCHISM – FREQUENTLY ASKED QUESTIONS

ISN'T ANARCHISM 'BAD'?

Unfortunately, the term has been degraded through mythology to mean "a world without rules" – usually garbed in post-apocalyptic outerwear and riding a well-armed motorbike. This is nonsense, of course. "Anarchy" is merely the logically consistent application of the moral premise that the initiation of the use of force is wrong. If violence is a bad way to solve problems, then the government is by definition immoral, since "government" always means a group of individuals who claim the right to initiate violence against everyone else, in the form of taxation, regulations etc.

BUT IF THERE IS NO GOVERNMENT, HOW CAN THE INEVITABLE CONFLICTS IN HUMAN SOCIETY BE RESOLVED?

The most important thing in philosophy is to consistently question the premises of propositions. For instance, embedded in the above question is the premise that conflicts within human society are currently being resolved by governments. This is pure nonsense. Governments are agencies of force – governments do not persuade, governments do not reason, governments do not motivate, governments do not encourage, governments do not resolve disputes. Governments have no more power to create morality then rape has to create love. A gun is only useful in self-defense; it cannot be used to create virtue.

FOR SOMEBODY WHO IS AN ANARCHIST, YOU SURE DO SOUND LIKE A POLITICIAN! WASN'T THAT JUST A COMPLETE DODGE OF THE QUESTION?

Excellent catch! Here is as good a place as any to introduce you to the concept of Dispute Resolution Organizations (DROs). This concept cannot answer every conceivable question you might have about dispute resolutions within a stateless society, but rather is a framework for understanding the *methodology* of dispute resolution – just as the scientific method cannot answer every possible question about the natural world, but rather points towards a methodology that allows those questions to be answered in a rational manner.

DROs are companies that specialize in insuring contracts between individuals, and resolving any disputes that might arise. For instance, if I borrow $1,000 from you, I may have to pay $10 to a DRO to insure my loan. If I fail to pay you back your money, the DRO will pay you instead. Obviously, as my credit rating improves, the cost of insuring my contracts will decline.

The DRO theory can be as complex as any other free market theory – and a lot of intellectual effort has gone into resolving how particular transactions might occur, such as multimillion dollar international contracts. Credible DRO theories have also been advanced that solve problems ranging from abortion to child abuse to murder to pollution. For more on DRO theory and practice, please see "The Stateless Society: An Examination of Alternatives" below.

BUT WHAT ABOUT THE ROADS?

The most important thing to understand about anarchism is that it is a moral theory which cannot logically be judged by consequences alone. For instance, the abolition of slavery was a moral imperative, because slavery as an institution is innately evil. The abolition of slavery was *not* conditional upon the provision of jobs for every freed slave. In a similar manner, anarchic theory does not have to explain how every conceivable social, legal or economic transaction could occur in the absence of a coercive government. What *is* important to understand is that the initiation of the use of force is a moral evil. With that in mind, we can approach the problem of roads more clearly.

First of all, roads are currently funded through the initiation of force. If you do not pay the taxes which support road construction, you will get a stern letter from the government, followed by a court date, followed by policemen coming to your house if you do not appear and submit to the court's judgment. If you use force to defend yourself against the policemen who are breaking into your home, you will very likely be shot down.

The roads, in other words, are built at the point of a gun. The use of violence is the central issue, not what might potentially happen in the absence of violence.

That having been said, roads will be built by housing developers, mall builders, those constructing schools and towns – just as they were before governments took them over in the 19th century. For more on this, please see the section on "Roads" below.

OKAY — HERE'S A SCENARIO FOR YOU: A GUY BUILDS A ROAD THAT COMPLETELY ENCIRCLES A SUBURBAN NEIGHBORHOOD, AND THEN CHARGES $1 MILLION FOR ANYONE TO CROSS THAT ROAD. ISN'T HE HOLDING EVERYONE WHO LIVES IN THAT NEIGHBORHOOD HOSTAGE?

This is fundamentally impossible. First of all, no one is going to buy a house in a neighborhood unless they are contractually guaranteed access to roads. Thus it will be impossible for anyone to completely encircle the neighborhood. Secondly, even if it *were* possible, it would be a highly risky investment. Can you imagine going to investors with a business plan that said: "I'm going to try to buy all the land that surrounds the neighborhood, and then charge exorbitant rates for anyone to cross that land." No sane investor would give you the money for such a plan. The risk of failure would be too great, and no DRO would enforce any contract that was so destructive, unpopular and economically unfeasible. DROs, unlike governments, must be appealing to the general population. If a DRO got involved with the encircling and imprisonment of a neighborhood, it would become so unpopular that it would lose far more business than it could potentially gain.

ALL RIGHT, SMARTY-PANTS — WHAT ABOUT THIS: THE COMPANY THAT SUPPLIES WATER TO A NEIGHBORHOOD SUDDENLY DECIDES TO INCREASE ITS RATES TENFOLD — PEOPLE ARE GOING TO BE FORCED TO PAY THE EXORBITANT PRICE, RIGHT?

First of all, if you are so concerned about people paying increasingly exorbitant prices for services, then it scarcely seems logical to propose the *government* as the solution to that problem! Taxes have risen immensely over the past 30 years, while services have declined.

However, even if we accept the premise of the problem, it is easily solved in a stateless society. First of all, no one will buy a house in a neighborhood without a contractual obligation that requires the supply of water at reasonable rates. Secondly, if the water company starts charging exorbitant prices, another company will simply move in and supply water in another form — in barrels, bottles or whatever. Thus, raising prices permanently costs the water company its customers — and makes every potential customer back away, for fear that the same predation will happen to them. Investors will quickly realize that the water company is shooting itself in the foot, and will align themselves with other shareholders, resulting in a takeover of the price-gouging water company, and a reduction in rates, accompanied by rank apologies and base groveling. Given that this result will be known in advance, no CEO would be allowed to pursue such a self-destructive course. Only governments that can be manipulated by corporations to prevent competition truly endanger consumers.

OKAY – WHAT IF TWO DROs HAVE DIFFERENT RULES – ISN'T THAT JUST GOING TO RESULT IN ENDLESS CIVIL WAR?

First of all, it is unlikely that DROs would have wildly different rules, because that would be economically inefficient. Cell phone companies use similar protocols, so that they can interoperate with each other. Railroad companies tend to use the same gauge, so that trains can travel as widely as possible. Internet service providers exchange data with other service providers, passing e-mails and other data back and forth. Like evolution, the free market is more about cooperation than pure competition. If a DRO wants to create a new rule, that rule will be fairly useless unless other DROs are willing to cooperate with it – just as a new e-mail program is fairly useless unless it uses existing protocols. This need for interoperability with other DROs will inevitably keep the number of new rules to the most economically efficient minimum. Customers will prefer DROs with broader reciprocity agreements, just as they prefer credit cards that are valid in a large number of locations.

New rules will also add to the costs for DRO subscribers – and if it costs them more money than it saves, the DRO will lose business.

BUT – WON'T THE MOST SUCCESSFUL DRO JUST ARM ITSELF, VIOLENTLY ELIMINATE ALL THE OTHER DROs, AND EMERGE AS A NEW GOVERNMENT?

First of all, if the potential emergence of a new government at some point in the future is of great concern, then surely the elimination of existing governments in the present is a worthy goal. If we have cancer, we go through chemotherapy to eliminate it in the present, even though we may get cancer again at some point in the future.

Secondly, unlike governments, DROs are not violent institutions. DROs will be primarily populated by white-collar workers: accountants, mediators, executives and so on. DROs are about as likely to become paramilitary organizations as your average accounting firm is likely to become an elite squad of ninja death warriors. Given the current existence of governments that possess nuclear weapons, I for one am willing to take that risk.

Thirdly, if a DRO tries to turn itself into a government, the other DROs will certainly act to prevent it. DROs would simply refuse to cooperate with any DRO that refused to submit to "arms inspections." Furthermore, DRO customers would also not take very kindly to their DRO becoming an armed institution – and their rates would certainly skyrocket, because their DRO would have to provide its regular services, as well as pay for all those black helicopters and RPGs. Any DRO that was paying for goods or services that its customers did not want – i.e. an army – would very quickly go out of business, because it would not be competitive in terms of rates. For more on this, please see "War, Profit and the State" below.

ARE THERE ANY EXAMPLES OF ANARCHIC SOCIETIES BEING SUCCESSFUL IN THE PAST?

There are, but that is not the essential question. Again, the essential aspect of anarchic theory is the moral rule banning the initiation of the use of force. Anarchists advocate a stateless society because governments are evil. When slavery was abolished for the first time in human history, there was no prior example of a successful slave–free society — if that had been a requirement, then slavery would be with us still.

That having been said, I can confidently point towards a nonviolent society that you're intimately aware of – *you*. I am guessing that you do not use violence directly to achieve your aims. It seems likely to me that you did not hold your employer hostage until you got your job; I also doubt that you keep your spouse locked in the basement, or that you threaten to shoot your "friends" if they do not join you on the dance floor. In other words, *you* are the perfect example of a stateless society. All of your personal relationships are voluntary, and do not involve the use of force. You are an anarchic microcosm – to see how a stateless society works, all you have to do is look in the mirror.

How can a society without a government pay for national defense? Many people, when first hearing the concept of a stateless society, cannot imagine how collective defense could possibly be paid for in the absence of taxation. I have already briefly discussed this above – here are some more details.

This is an important question to ask, but there is a way of answering it that also answers many other questions about collective action.

In any society, there are four possibilities that can occur in the realm of collective defense. The first is that *no one* wants to pay for collective defense. The second is that only a *minority* of people want to pay for collective defense; the third is that the *majority* of people want to pay for collective defense; and the fourth is that *everyone* wants to pay for collective defense.

Let's compare how these four possibilities play out in a state-based democracy:

1. *No one wants to pay for collective defense.* In this case, voters will universally reject any politician who proposes collective defense of any kind.
2. *Only a minority of people want to pay for collective defense.* In this case, no politician who proposes paying for collective defense will ever get into office, because he will never secure a majority of the votes.
3. *The majority of people want to pay for collective defense.* In this case, pro-defense politicians will be voted into office, and spend tax money on defense.
4. *Everyone wants to pay for collective defense.* This achieves the same outcome as number three.

Thus, all other things being equal, *a democracy produces almost the same outcome as a stateless society* – with the important exception of #2. If only a minority of people want to pay for defense, they cannot do so in a democracy, but can do so in a stateless society.

In a stateless society, if the majority of people are interested in paying for collective defense, it will be paid for. The addition of the government to the interaction is entirely superfluous – the equivalent of creating a Ministry devoted to communicating the pleasures of candy to children, or sex to teenagers.

However, the possibility exists that people are willing to pay for collective defense only if they know that everyone *else* is paying for it as well. This argument fails on multiple levels, both empirical and rational.

1. People tip waiters and give to charity, even though they know that some people never do.
2. There is no reason why, in a stateless society, people should not have full knowledge of who has donated to collective defense. Agencies providing collective defense could easily issue a "donor card," which certain shops or employers might ask to see before doing business. Names of donors could also be put on a website, easily searchable, creating social pressures to donate.
3. When the money required for collective defense is stripped from taxpayers at the point of a gun, a basic moral tenet – and rational criterion – is violated. Citizens institute collective defense in order to protect their property – it makes no sense whatsoever to create an agency to protect property rights and then invest that agency with the power to violate property rights at will.
4. When collective defense is paid for by the initiation of the use of force, there is no rational ceiling to costs, and no incentive for efficiency – thus ensuring that costs will escalate to the point where they become unsustainable, causing a collapse of the economic system and leaving the country vulnerable.

WHAT ABOUT EDUCATION?

The question of education follows the same pattern as the question of collective defense outlined above. However, there are certain additional pieces of information that can strengthen the case for a free market in education.

First of all, it is important understand that State education was not imposed because children were not being educated. Prior to the institution of government-run education, the functional literacy rate of the average American was over 90% – *far* better than it is now, after hundreds of billions of dollars have been spent "educating" children. Before the government forcefully took over the schools, there was almost no violence in schools, there were no school shootings, no violent gangs, no assaults on teachers – and it did not take more than two decades and hundreds of thousands of dollars to produce a reasonably-educated adult. Most of the intellectual giants of the 18th and 19th centuries – the Founding Fathers included – did not even finish high school, let alone go to college.

Government education in America was instituted as a means of cultural control, due to rising tribal fears about the growing number of non-Protestants in society – the "immigrant issue" of the time.

There are a number of core reasons that government education cripples children's minds; for the sake of brevity, we will deal with only one here.

It is reasonable to assume that the majority of parents want to give their children a good education – and this education must necessarily include the teaching of values, or the relationship between personal ethics and real-world choices. In any multicultural society, however, a common curriculum *cannot include any fundamental values*, for fear of offending various groups. Thus values must be stripped from education, turning its focus to rote memorization, bland technical skills (geometry, sports, wood shop), and neutral and propagandistic views of society and politics ("Democracy is good!" "Respect multiculturalism!" "Reduce, Reuse, Recycle!"). This effectively kills the energetic curiosity of the young, turns school into a mind-numbing series of empty exercises, creates frustration among those needing stimulation, and engenders deep disrespect for the educational system – and its teachers – who remain institutionally indifferent to the welfare of the students. Combine this hostility and frustration with the easy money available through drug sales – and the possibility of surviving on welfare – and entire generations of youths become mentally crippled. The costs of this are beyond calculation, since the damage goes far beyond economics.

YES, BUT HOW WILL POOR CHILDREN GET AN EDUCATION IF IT IS NOT PAID FOR THROUGH TAXES?

This reminds me of the old Soviet cartoon – two old women are standing in an endless line-up to buy bread. One says to the other: "What a terribly long line!" The other replies: "Yes, but just imagine – in the capitalist countries, the government doesn't even *distribute* the bread!"

Whenever I argue for a stateless society, I say: "The government should not provide 'X'." The response always comes back: "But how will 'X' then be provided?"

As mentioned above, the answer is simple: "Since everybody is concerned that 'X' will not be provided, 'X' will naturally be provided by those who are concerned by its absence." In other words, since everyone is concerned that poor children might not get an education because it costs too much, *those children will be provided an education as a direct result of everyone's concern.*

Look, either you will help poor children get an education, through charity or volunteering, or you will not. If you *will* help poor children get an education, you do not have to worry about the issue. If you will do nothing to help poor children get an education, it is pure hypocrisy to raise it as an issue that you claim to be concerned about.

That having been said, there are a number of ways that a free society can provide education that is far superior to the mess being inflicted on children now.

First of all, poor children *are not currently getting any sort of decent education.* The perceived risks of a stateless society cannot be rationally compared to a perfect situation in the here-and-now. Those most concerned with the education of the poor should be the ones most clamouring for the abolishment of the existing system. The educational statistics for poor children are absolutely appalling – and this should raise the urgency of finding a solution. It is one thing to say, "You should never cross a road against the lights, even if there is no traffic." It is quite another thing to say, "You should never cross a road against the lights, even if you are being chased by a lion!" Those who oppose a stateless society always ignore the existence of the lion, thus adding their intellectual inertia to the weight of the status quo.

Secondly, much like the question of collective defense, the cost of education will be far lower in a free society. The $10,000-$15,000 a year currently being spent per-pupil in public schools is ridiculously overinflated. Year-round accelerated education would help the child graduate several years earlier – and with tangible job skills to boot! The resulting increase in earnings would more than pay for the education – and many companies would scramble to offer loans to such children, knowing that they would be paid off soon after graduation. Thus education would be more beneficial – and, since there would be no war on drugs or automatic "welfare" in a free society, fewer self-destructive options would be available.

As for higher education, it is either recreational or vocational. If it is recreational, then it is about as necessary as a hobby, and cannot be considered a necessity. If it is vocational, such as medicine, then additional earnings will more than pay for the costs of the education. Businesses need accountants – thus those businesses will be more than happy to fund the college expenses of talented youngsters in return for a work commitment after graduation. (This is how my father received his doctorate.)

Talented but poor children will be sought after by schools, both for the benevolence they can show by subsidizing them, and also because high-quality graduates raise the prestige of a school, enabling it to increase fees.

In a stateless society, a tiny minority of poor children may slip through the cracks – but that is far better than the current situation, where *most* poor children slip through the cracks. The fact that some non-smokers will get lung cancer does not mean that we should encourage people to smoke. A stateless society is not a utopia, it is merely a utopia compared to a government society.

Now, we shall really begin to make the case for anarchism by examining the question of whether the government is a valid moral entity.

Disproving the State: Four Arguments Against Government

Two objections constantly tend to recur whenever the subject of dissolving the State arises. The first is that a free society is only possible if people are perfectly good or rational. In other words, citizens need a centralized State because there are evil people in the world.

The first and most obvious problem with this position is that if evil people exist in society, they will also exist within the State – and be far more dangerous thereby. Citizens are able to protect themselves against evil individuals, but stand no chance against an aggressive State armed to the teeth with police and military might. Thus, the argument that we need the State because evil people exist is false. If evil people exist, the State *must* be dismantled, since evil people will be drawn to use its power for their own ends – and, unlike private thugs, evil people in government have the police and military to inflict their whims on a helpless and largely disarmed population.

Logically, there are four possibilities as to the mixture of good and evil people in the world:

1. That all men are moral;
2. That all men are immoral;
3. That the majority of men are moral, and a minority immoral;
4. That the majority of men are immoral, and a minority moral.

(A perfect balance of good and evil is statistically impossible.)

In the first case, (all men are moral), the State is obviously unnecessary, since evil does not exist.

In the second case, (all men are immoral), the State cannot be permitted to exist for one simple reason. The State, it is generally argued, must exist because there are evil people in the world who desire to inflict harm, and who can only be restrained through fear of State retribution (police, prisons etc). A corollary of this argument is that the less retribution these people fear, the more evil they will do. However, the State itself is not subject to any force, but is a law unto itself. Even in Western democracies, how many policemen and politicians go to jail? Thus if evil people wish to do harm but are only restrained by force, then society can never permit a State to exist, because evil people will immediately take control of that State, in order to do evil and avoid retribution. In a society of pure evil, then, the only hope for stability would be a state of nature, where a general arming and fear of retribution would blunt the evil intents of disparate groups.

The third possibility is that most people are evil, and only a few are good. If this is the case, then the State *also* cannot be permitted to exist, since the majority of those in control of the State will be evil, and will rule over the good minority. Democracy in particular cannot be permitted to exist, since the minority of good people would be subjugated to the democratic will of the evil majority. Evil people, who wish to do harm without fear of retribution, would inevitably take control of the State, and use its power to do their evil free of that fear. Good people act morally because they love virtue and peace of mind, not because they fear retribution – and thus, unlike evil people, they have little to gain by controlling the State. And so it is certain that the State will be controlled by a majority of evil people who will rule over all, to the detriment of all moral people.

The fourth option is that most people are good, and only a few are evil. This possibility is subject to the same problems outlined above, notably that evil people will always want to gain control over the State, in order to shield themselves from retaliation. This option changes the appearance of democracy, of course: because the majority of people are good, evil power-seekers must lie to them in order to gain power, and then, after achieving public office, will immediately break faith and pursue their own corrupt agendas, enforcing their wills with the police and military. (This is the current situation in democracies, of course.) Thus the State remains the greatest prize to the most evil men, who will quickly gain control over its awesome power – to the detriment of all good souls – and so the State cannot be permitted to exist in this scenario either.

It is clear, then, that there is no situation under which a State can logically or morally be allowed to exist. The only possible justification for the existence of a State would be if the majority of men are evil, but all the power of the State is always controlled by a minority of good men. This situation, while interesting theoretically, breaks down logically because:

a.   The evil majority would quickly outvote the minority or overpower them through a coup;

b.   Because there is no way to ensure that only good people would always run the State; and,

c.   There is absolutely no example of this having ever occurred in any of the dark annals of the brutal history of the State.

The logical error always made in the defense of the State is to imagine that any collective moral judgments being applied to any group of people *is not also being applied to the group which rules over them.* If 50% of citizens are evil, then at least 50% of the people ruling over them are *also* evil (and probably more, since evil people are always drawn to power). Thus the existence of evil can never justify the existence of the State. If there is no evil, the State is unnecessary. If evil exists, the State is far too dangerous to be allowed existence.

Why is this error always made? There are a number of reasons, which can only be touched on here. The first is that the State introduces itself to children in the form of public school teachers who are considered moral authorities. Thus is the association of morality and authority with the State first made, and is reinforced through years of repetition. The second is that the State never teaches children about the root of its power – force – but instead pretends that it is just another social institution, like a business or a church or a charity. The third is that the prevalence of religion has always blinded men to the evils of the State – which is why the State has always been so interested in furthering the interests of churches. In the religious world-view, absolute power is synonymous with perfect goodness, in the form of a deity. In the real political world of men, however, increasing power always means increasing evil. With religion, also, all that happens must be for the good – thus, fighting encroaching political power is fighting the will of the deity. There are many more reasons, of course, but these are among the deepest.

I mentioned at the beginning of this section that people generally make *two* errors when confronted with the idea of dissolving the State. The first is believing that the State is necessary because evil people exist. The second is the belief that, in the absence of a State, any social institutions which arise will inevitably take the place of the State. Thus, Dispute Resolution Organizations (DROs), insurance companies and private security forces are all considered potential cancers which will swell and overwhelm the body politic.

This view arises from the same error outlined above. If all social institutions are constantly trying to grow in power and enforce their wills on others, then *by that very argument a centralized State cannot be allowed to exist*. If it is an iron law that groups always try to gain power over other groups and individuals, then that power-lust will not end if one of them wins, but will spread across society until slavery is the norm.

It is also very hard to understand the logic and intelligence of the argument that, in order to protect us from a group that might overpower us, we should support a group that has already overpowered us. It is similar to the statist argument about private monopolies – that citizens should create a State monopoly because they are afraid of a private monopoly.

Once we begin to reason away the fogs of propaganda, it does not take keen vision to see through such nonsense.

ANARCHY, VIOLENCE AND THE STATE

DOES MORE GOVERNMENT EQUAL LESS VIOLENCE?
Another common objection to a stateless society is that violence will inevitably increase in the absence of a centralized State. This is a very interesting objection, and

seems to arise from people who have imbibed a large amount of propaganda about the nature and function of the State. It seems hard to imagine that this conclusion could ever be reached by reasoning from first principles, as we will see below.

There are several circumstances under which the use of violence will either increase, or decrease – and they tend to correspond with the basic principles of economics. For instance, people tend to respond to incentives, and tend to be drawn to circumstances under which they can gain the most resources by expending the least effort. Thus in the lottery system, people respond to the incentive of the million dollar payout by expending minimal resources in the purchase of a ticket.

There are several circumstances under which violence will tend to increase, rather than decrease – and interestingly enough, a centralized State creates and exacerbates all such circumstances.

Principle 1: Risk

Economically speaking, risk is the great balancer of reward. If a horse is less likely to win a race, the gambling payout must be higher in order to induce people to bet on it. By their very nature, speculative investments must potentially produce greater rewards than blue-chip stocks. Similarly, white-collar criminals generally face less physical risk than muggers. A stick-up man may inadvertently run up against a judo expert, and find the tables turned very quickly – while a hacker siphoning off funds electronically faces no such risk. In general, those interested in stealing property will always gravitate toward situations where the risks of retaliation are lower.

If force or the threat thereof is required for the theft – as in the case of taxes – one of the greatest ways of reducing the possibilities of retaliation is through the principle of overwhelming force. If five enormous muggers circle a 98 pound man and demand his wallet, the possibilities of retaliation are far lower than if the 98 pound man approaches five enormous men and demands that they surrender *their* wallets.

Clearly, the existence of a centralized State creates such an enormous disparity of power that resistance against government predations is, in all practicality, impossible.

A man can either stand up to or move away from the Mafia, but can do almost nothing to oppose expansions of State power.

Thus, we can see that the existence of a centralized State creates the following problems with regards to violence:

1. The use of violence tends to increase when the risks of using that violence decrease;
2. The risks of initiating violence tend to decrease as the disparity of power increases;
3. There is no greater disparity of power than that between a citizen and his government;
4. Therefore there is no better way to increase the use of violence than to create a centralized political state.

Principle 2: Proximity

Using violence is a brutal and horrible task for most people. Most people are not physically or mentally equipped to use violence, either due to a lack of physical strength, a lack of martial knowledge, or an absence of sociopathic tendencies. However, the government has enormous, relatively efficient and well-distributed systems in place to initiate the use of force against largely disarmed citizens. Thus, those who wish to gain the fruits of violence can do so by tapping into the government's network of enforcers, without ever having to directly witness or deploy violence themselves.

It can generally be said that the use of violence tends to increase as the visibility and proximity of violence decreases. In other words, if you can get other people to do your dirty work, more dirty work will tend to get done. If everyone who wished to gain the fruits of State violence had to hold their own guns to everyone's heads, almost all of them would end up refraining from such direct and dangerous brutality.

Thus in the realm of proximity as well, the existence of a centralized State tends to both distance and hide the reality of violence from those who wish to pluck the fruits of violence – thus ensuring that the use of violence will tend to increase.

PRINCIPLE 3: EXTERNALIZATION OF COSTS

In a stateless society, it is impossible to "outsource" violence to the police or the military, since they are not funded through collective coercion. When there is a government, however, those who wish to gain the fruits of violence – i.e. tax revenues, the regulation of competitors, the blocking of imports and so on – can lobby the government to enforce such beneficial restrictions on the free trade and choices of others. They will have to pay for this lobbying effort, but they will not have to directly fund the police and the military and the court system and the prison guards in order to force people to obey their whims. This "externalization of costs" is an essential ingredient in the expansion of the use of violence.

For instance, imagine you are a steel manufacturer who wants to block the imports of steel from other countries – how expensive would it be to build your own navy, your own radar system, your own Coast Guard, hire your own inspectors and so on? How would you convince all the shippers and dock owners and transporters to inspect every container on your behalf? Would you pay them? Would you threaten them? And even if you found it economically advantageous to do all *that*, could you guarantee that none of your competitors would do the same? Would it still be economically advantageous if you ended up getting into an arms race with all of your fellow manufacturers? And what if your customers found out that you were using your own private militia to block the imports of steel – might they not take offense at your use of violence and boycott you? No, in the absence of a centralized State that you can offload all the enforcement costs to, it is going to be far cheaper for you to compete openly than develop your own private, overwhelming and universal army.

Thus, in any situation where the costs of using violence can be externalized to some centralized agency, the use of that violence will always tend to increase. Offloading the costs of violence to taxpayers will always make violence profitable to specific agencies – whether private or public. And so, once again, we can see that the existence of the State will always tend to increase the use of violence.

PRINCIPLE 4: DEFERMENT

How much do you think you would spend if you knew that you would be long-dead when the bill came due? This is, of course, the basic principle of deficit financing – the deferment of payments to the next generation – which is perhaps the most insidious form of taxation. Forcibly transferring property from those who have not even been born yet is perhaps the greatest "externalization" of costs that can be imagined! Naturally, the risks of retaliation from the unborn are utterly nonexistent – and neither is any direct violence performed against them. Thus the principle of "deferment" is perhaps one of the greatest ways in which the existence of a centralized State increases the use of violence.

PRINCIPLE 5: PROPAGANDA

It is well known in totalitarian regimes that in order to get people to accept the use of violence, that violence must always be reframed in a noble light. Government violence can never be referred to as merely the use of brute force for the material gain of politicians and bureaucrats – it must always represent the manifestation of core social or cultural values, such as caring for the poor, the sick, the old, or the indigent. The violence must always be tucked away from direct view, and the effects of violence elevated to sentimental heights of soaring rhetoric. Furthermore, the effects of the withdrawal of violence must always be portrayed as catastrophic and evil. Thus the elimination of the welfare state would cause mass starvation; the elimination of medical subsidies would cause mass death; the elimination of the war on drugs would cause massive addictions and social collapse – and the elimination of the State *itself* would directly create a post-apocalyptic cyberpunk nightmare world of brutal and endlessly warring gangs.

Propaganda is different from advertising in that all that advertising can ever do is get you to try a product for the first time – if the quality of the product does not meet your needs or expectations, then you will simply never buy that product again. Propaganda, on the other hand, is quite different. Advertising appeals to choice and self-interest; propaganda uses rhetoric to morally justify the *absence* of choice and self-interest. Advertising can only stimulate a one-time demand; propaganda permanently suppresses rationality. Advertising generally uses the argument from effect (you will be better off); propaganda always uses the argument from morality (you are evil for doubting).

The private funding of propaganda is never economically viable, since the amount of time and energy required to instil propaganda in the mind of the average person is far too great to justify its cost. In a voluntary system like the free market, paying for year after year of propaganda (which can only result in a "first time" purchase of a good or service) is never worth it. Propaganda is only "worth it" when it can be used to keep people passive within a coercive system like State taxation or regulation. For instance, here in Canada, socialized medicine is always called a "core Canadian value," and can be subject to no rational, moral or economic analysis. (Of course, if it really *were* a "core Canadian value," we would scarcely need the State to enforce it!) Because the existing system is so terrible, it takes years of State propaganda – primarily directed at children – to overcome people's *actual* experiences of the endless disasters of socialized medicine. Propaganda is always required where people would never voluntarily choose the situation that the propaganda is praising. Thus we need endless propaganda extolling the virtues of the welfare state, the war on drugs and socialized medicine, while the virtues of eating chocolate cake are left for us to discover and maintain on our own.

Government propaganda is primarily aimed at children through State schools, and usually takes the form of an *absence* of topics. The coercive nature of the State is never mentioned, of course, and neither are the financial benefits which accrue to those who control the State. Children *do* hear endlessly about how the State protects the environment, feeds the poor and heals the sick. This propaganda blinds people to the true nature of State violence – thus ensuring that State violence can increase with relatively little or no opposition.

Parents are forced to pay for the propaganda of public schools through taxation. Thus a ghastly situation is created wherein the taxpayers are forced to pay for their own indoctrination – and the indoctrination of their children. This "externalization of cost" is perhaps the greatest tool that the government uses to ensure that increasing State violence will be subject to little or no opposition or rational analysis. No corporation or private agency could possibly profit from a 14-year program of indoctrinating children – the State, however, by inflicting the costs of indoctrination onto parents, creates a situation where the slaves are forced to pay for their own manacles. And as we all know, when slaves don't resist, owning slaves becomes economically far more viable.

For the above reasons, it is clear that the existence of a centralized State vastly increases both the profits and the prevalence of violence. The fact that the violence is masked by obedience in no way diminishes the brutality of coercion. All moralists interested in one of the greatest topics of ethics – the reduction or elimination of violence – would do well to understand the depth and degree to which the existence of a centralized State promotes, exacerbates – and profits from – violence. Private violence is a negative but manageable situation – however, as we can see from countless examples throughout history, public violence always escalates until civil society becomes seriously threatened. Because the State so directly profits from violence, eliminating the State can in no way increase the use of violence within society. Quite the contrary – since private agencies do not profit from violence, eliminating the State will, to a degree unprecedented in human history, eliminate violence as well.

WAR, PROFIT AND THE STATE

It has often been said that *war is the health of the State* – but the argument could also be made that the reverse is more true: that *the State is the health of war*. In other words, that war – the greatest of all human evils – is impossible without the State.

The great Austrian economist Ludwig von Mises was once asked what the central defining characteristic of the free market was – i.e. since every economy is more or less a mixture of freedom and State compulsion, what institution truly separated a free market from a controlled economy – and he replied that it was the existence of a stock market. Through a stock market, entrepreneurs can achieve the *externalization of risk*, or the partial transfer of potential losses from themselves to investors. In the absence of this capacity, business growth is almost impossible.

In other words, when risk is reduced, demand increases. The stagnation of economies in the absence of a stock market is testament to the unwillingness of individuals to take on *all* the risks of an economic endeavour themselves, even if this were possible. When risk becomes *sharable*, new possibilities emerge that were not present before – the Industrial Revolution being perhaps the most dramatic example.

Sadly, one of those possibilities – in all its horror, corruption, brutality and genocide – is war. In this section, I will endeavour to show that, in its capacity to reduce the costs and risks of violence, the State is, in effect, *the stock market of war.*

All economists know the "fallacy of the broken window," which is that the stimulation of demand caused by a vandal breaking a window does not *add* to economic growth, but rather subtracts from it, since the money spent replacing the window is deducted from other possible purchases. This is self-evident to all of us – we don't try to increase our incomes by driving our cars off cliffs or burning down our houses. Although it might please car manufacturers and home builders, it neither pleases us, nor the people who would have had access to the new car and house if we did not need them for ourselves. Destruction always diverts resources and so bids up prices, which costs everyone.

(In fact, breaking a $100 window removes *more* than $100 from the economy, since all the time spent returning the window to its original state – calling the window repairman, deciding on the replacement, cleaning up the shards of glass, etc – is also subtracted from the economy as a whole.)

There will always be accidents, of course, and so repairs are a legitimate aspect of any free market. However, war can *never* be said to be an accident, is never part of the free market, and yet is commonly believed to be good for the economy – and must be, for at least some people, since it is pursued so often. How can these opposites be reconciled? How can destruction be economically advantageous, when it is so obviously bad for the economy as a whole?

We can imagine an unethical window repairman who smashes windows in order to raise demand for his business. This would certainly help his income – and yet we see that this course is almost never pursued in real life in the free market. Why not?

One obvious answer could be that business managers are afraid of going to jail – and that certainly *is* a risk, but not a very great one. Arsonists are notoriously hard to catch, for instance, and there are so many hard-to-trace sabotages that can be undertaken. Poison can be added to the water supply that would incriminate a water supplier, which would take months to resolve – at which point the trail would be long cold. Foreign hackers could be paid to infiltrate competitor's networks, or mount denial-of-service attacks on their web sites – sure doom for those who sell over the Internet.

Not convinced? Well, what about eBay? If you have a competitor who is taking away your business, why not just get a hundred of your closest friends to give him a bad rating, and watch his reputation – and business – dry up and blow away?

All of the above practices are very rare in the free market, for three main reasons. The first is that they are costly; the second is that they increase risks, and the third is the fear of retaliation.

THE COST OF DESTRUCTION

If you want to hire an arsonist to torch the factory of your competitor, you have to become an expert in underworld negotiations. You might pay an arsonist and watch him take off to Hawaii instead of setting the fire. You also face the risk that your arsonist will take your offer to your competitor and ask for more money to *not* set the fire – or, worse, return the favor and torch your factory! It will certainly cost money to start down the road of vandalism, and there is no guarantee that your investment will pay off in the way you want.

There are other tertiary costs to pursuing a path of "competition by destruction." You can only target one competitor at a time, which is only partially helpful, since most businesses face many competitors simultaneously – some local, and some overseas and probably out of reach. Even if you are successful in destroying your competitor, you have opened a "hole" in the market, which will just invite others to come in – and perhaps compete even more fiercely with you. When it comes to competition, in most cases it is better to stay with "the devil you know." It wouldn't make much sense to knock out a small software competitor, for instance, and end up giving Microsoft a good reason to enter the market.

Also, if you are a business owner, competition is very good for you. Just as a sports team gets lazy and unskilled if it never plays a competent opponent, businesses without competition get unproductive, lazy and inefficient – a sure invitation to others to come in and compete. Successful businesses *need* competition to stay fit. Resistance breeds strength.

Also, what happens if you *do* manage to successfully sabotage your opponents? If you do it well, no one has any idea that you are behind the sudden spate of arson. What happens to your insurance costs? They go through the roof – if you can even get any! Furthermore, you will not be able to meet all the new demand right away, thus ensuring that clients will find alternatives, which will likely remain outside your control. Thus you have increased your costs, created incentives for potential customers to find alternatives and alarmed your employees – creating a dangerous situation where competitors are highly motivated to enter your field just when you are the most vulnerable to competition! Overall, not a very bright idea!

The Risks of Destruction

Let us say you decide to pay a man named Stan to torch your competitor's factory – well, the basic reality of the transaction is that Stan, as a professional arsonist, knows how to work the situation to his advantage far better than you do, since you are, ahem, new to the field. Stan knows that no matter what he does, you cannot go to the police for protection. What if he tapes your conversations and then blackmails you? Then your exercise in amoral competition suddenly becomes a lifelong nightmare of expense, guilt, fear and rage.

As mentioned above, what if Stan decides to go to your competitor and reveal your plans? Surely your competitor would pay good money for that information, since he could then go to the police and destroy you legally even more completely than you were hoping to destroy him illegally. A basic fact of criminal activity is that once the gloves come off, the results become very hard to predict indeed!

What if Stan goes to your competitor and says: "For $25,000, I was supposed to torch this place – for $30,000 I can just turn around and set quite a different fire!" This pendulum bidding war can turn into a desperately stressful money-loser for everyone concerned (except Stan, of course).

And who is to say that Stan is even a "legitimate" arsonist? What if he is an undercover agent of some kind? What if he has been sent by someone else in order to get some dirt on you? What if it turns out to be blackmail, or a set-up by your competitor? How would you know? Again – it is all very risky!

THE RISKS OF PERSONAL RETALIATION

Let us say that all of the above works out just the way you want it and Stan actually torches your competitor Bill's factory – what might happen then? You have just created a bitter enemy who suspects foul play, knows that you have a good motive for torching his factory, and has nothing to lose. He might complain about you to the police, hire private investigators and put an ad in every local paper offering a cash reward of a million dollars for information leading to proof of your participation – so he can sue you and recover far more than a million dollars!

Either your new enemy will find out actionable information, and then go to the police, or he will find out *unactionable* information – hints, not proof – in which case he may choose to retaliate against you. Since you've been able to do it in a way that cannot be proven – and he now knows how – you have just educated a bitter and angry man on how to torch a factory and escape detection. Are you going to sleep safe in your bed? Are you sure that he's going to target only your *factory*?

What does all this look like in terms of *economic* calculation? Have a look at a sample table below showing the costs and benefits of competition through arson. If we assign arson a cost of $50k, with a 50% probability of success, and a resulting economic benefit of $1m, we see a net benefit of $450k (50% of $1m – $50k in costs). So far so good. But if we include a 10% risk of blackmail, a 20% chance of retaliation, a 25% chance of increased competition – all reasonable numbers – and finally $100k in increased insurance and security costs – we can see that the economic benefits are erased very quickly (see below).

Action	Cost	Probability	Economic Effect	Net Benefits (benefit / risk – cost)
Arson	-$50k	50%	$1 mill	$450k
Blackmail	-$250k	10%	-$250k	-$25k
Retaliation	-$1 mill	20%	-$1 mill	-$200k
Increased Competition	-$500k	25%	-$500k	-$125k
Increased Costs (insurance, security)	-$100k	100%	-$100k	-$100k
			Net Effect	$0

(Note that the above table only shows the economic calculations – these do not include the emotional factors of guilt, fear and worry, which are of great significance but hard to quantify. This is important because even if the above numbers were less disagreeable, the emotional barrier would still have to be overcome.)

As the above conservative example shows, it is not really worth it to attempt economic gain through the destruction of property – and that is exactly how it should be.

We want people to be good, of course, but we also want strong economic incentives for virtue as well, to shore up the uncertain integrity of free will!

How does this relate to war and the State? Very closely, in fact – but with very opposite effects.

The Economics of War

The economics of war are, at bottom, very simple, and contain three major players: those who *decide* on war, those who *profit* from war, and those who *pay* for war. Those who decide on war are the politicians, those who profit from it are those who supply military materials or are paid for military skills, and those who pay for war are the taxpayers. (The first and second groups, of course, overlap.)

In other words, a corporation which profits from supplying arms to the military is paid through a predation on citizens through State taxation – and under no other circumstances could the transaction exist, since the risks associated with destruction outlined above are equal to or greater than any profits that could be made.

Certainly if those who *decided* on war also *paid* for it, there would be no such thing as war, since war follows the same economic incentives and costs outlined above.

However, those who decide on war do not pay for it – that unpleasant task is relegated to the taxpayers (both current, in the form of direct taxes and inflation, and future, in the form of national debts).

Let us see how the above analysis of the costs of destruction changes when the State enters the equation.

The Costs of Military Destruction

If you want to start a war, you need a very expensive military – which must also be trained and maintained when there is no war. There is simply no way to recover the costs of that military by invading another country – otherwise, the free market would directly fund armies and invasions, which it never does. Or, if you would prefer another way of looking at it, you can only invade another country by destroying large portions of it, killing many of its citizens, and then fighting endless insurgencies. Given the costs of invasions and occupations – always in the hundreds of millions or billions of dollars – what profits could conceivably be extracted from the bombed-out country you are occupying? That would be like asking a thief to make money by fire-bombing a house he wanted to steal from, and then staying and keeping the occupants hostage. Madness! Thieves don't operate that way – and neither would war, without the presence of the State and the money of the taxpayers.

Since the taxpayer's money pays for the war, the costs of destruction for those who start the war are very low – how much does George Bush *personally* pay for the Iraq invasion? While it is true that those who profit from the war also pay the taxes needed to support the war effort, the amount they pay in taxes is far less than they receive in profits – again, facts we know because there are always people willing and eager to supply the military.

THE RISKS OF ANNIHILATION

Those who decide on war and those who profit from war only start wars when there is no real risk of personal destruction. This is a simple historical fact, which can be gleaned from the reality that no nuclear power has ever declared war on another nuclear power. The US gave the USSR money and wheat, and yet invaded Grenada, Haiti and Iraq. (In fact, one of the central reasons it was possible to know in advance that Iraq had no weapons of mass destruction capable of hitting the US was that US leaders were willing to invade it.)

Avoiding the risk of destruction was the reason that the USSR and the US (to take two obvious examples) fought "proxy wars" in out-of-the-way places like Afghanistan, Vietnam and Korea. As we shall see below, the fact that the risk of destruction is shifted to taxpayers (and taxpayer-funded soldiers) considerably changes the economic equation.

The Risks of Military Retaliation

The "risk of retaliation" in economic calculations regarding war should not be taken as a *general* risk, but rather a *specific* one – i.e. specific to those who either decide on war or profit from it. For example, Roosevelt knew that blockading Japan in the early 1940s carried a grave risk of retaliation – but only against distant and unknown US personnel in the Pacific, not against his friends and family in Washington. (In fact, the blockading was specifically escalated with the aim of provoking retaliation, in order to bring the US into WWII.)

If *other people* are exposed to the risk of retaliation, the risk becomes a moot point from an amoral economic standpoint. If I smoke, but some unknown stranger *might* get lung cancer, my decision to continue smoking will certainly be affected!

Externalizing Military Risk

The power of the State to so fundamentally shift the costs and benefits of violence is one of the most central facts of warfare – and the core reason for its continued existence. As we can see from the above table regarding arson, if the person who decides to profit through destruction faces the consequences *himself,* he has almost no economic incentive to do so. However, if he can shift the risks and losses to others – but retain the benefit himself – the economic landscape changes completely! Sadly, it then it becomes profitable, say, to tax citizens to pay for 800 US military bases around the world, as long as strangers in New York bear the brunt of the inevitable retaliation. It also becomes profitable to send uneducated youngsters to Iraq to bear the brunt of the insurgency.

Externalizing Emotional Discomfort

The fact that the State shifts the burden of risk and payment to the taxpayers and soldiers is very important in emotional terms. If the "arson" example could be tweaked to provide a profit – say, by reducing the risks of blackmail or retaliation – the other risks would still accrue to the man contemplating such violence. Such risks would cause emotional discomfort in all but the most rare and sociopathic personalities – and the generation of negative stimuli such as fear, guilt and worry would *still* require more profit than the model can reasonably generate.

Thus the fact that the State externalizes almost *all* the risks and costs of destruction is a *further* positive motivation to those who would use the power of State violence for their own ends. Once you throw in endless pro-war propaganda (also called "war-nography"), the emotional benefits of starting and leading wars funded by others can become a definitive positive – which ensures that wars will continue until the State collapses, or the world dies.

In Other Words, The State Is War

If the above is understood, then the hostility of anarchists towards the State should now be at least a little clearer. In the anarchist view, the State is a fundamental moral evil not only because it uses violence to achieve its ends, but also because it is the only social agency capable of making war economically advantageous to those with the power to declare it and profit from it. In other words, it is only through the governmental power of taxation that war can be subsidized to the point where it becomes profitable to certain sections of society. Destruction can only ever be profitable because the costs and risks of violence are shifted to the taxpayers, while the benefits accrue to the few who directly control or influence the State.

This violent distortion of costs, incentives and rewards cannot be controlled or alleviated, since an artificial imbalance of economic incentives will always self-perpetuate and escalate (at least, until the inevitable bankruptcy of the public purse). Or, to put it another way, as long as the State exists, we shall always live with the terror of war. To oppose war is to oppose the State. They can neither be examined in isolation nor opposed separately, since – much more than metaphorically – the State and war are two sides of the same bloody coin.

A Successful Operation (a dead patient!)

Most libertarians have, at one time or another, been challenged by the problem of *public property,* or how the market can best protect and allocate goods "owned" in common such as fish in the sea, roads, airwaves and so on. An old economics parable sums up the problem nicely – let's briefly review it before taking a strong swing at solving the problem of public property.

The issue is well described by a parable called *the problem of the commons* (POTC), which goes something like this: a group of sheep-owning farmers own land in a ring around a common area. They each benefit individually from letting their sheep graze on the common land, since that frees up some of their own farmland for other uses. However, if they *all* let their sheep graze on the commons, they all suffer, since the land will be stripped bare, and so they will end up watching their sheep starve, since their *own* land has all been turned to other uses. In many circles, this is considered an incontrovertible *coup de grace* for the absolute right of private property – and the free market in general – insofar as it "proves" that individual self-interest, rationally pursued, can result in economic catastrophe. Due to the POTC, it is argued, the property rights of the individual must be curtailed for the sake of the "greater good." Thus regulation and government ownership must be instituted to control the excesses of individual self-interest for the sake of long-term stability, blah blah blah.

There is one significant difficulty with the POTC, however, which is that it fails to prove that government regulation or public ownership is necessary, or that turning the POTC over to the State solves the problem in any way. In fact, it is easy to prove that even if the POTC *is* a real dilemma, *the worst possible way of solving it is to create government regulations or public ownership.*

PROBLEM #1: PUBLIC OWNERSHIP

The simplest rebuttal to the POTC, of course, is to point out that the problem faced by the farmers is not an *excess* of private property, but a *deficiency*. If we imagine the farms surrounding the commons to be doughnut-shaped, then clearly the POTC is best solved by simply extending the ownership of the farms to the very center, like pizza slices (yes, these metaphors are making me hungry as well!). If private property is thus extended to *include* the commons, farmers no longer face the problem of everyone wanting to exploit un-owned resources. Everyone can then use their extra land to feed their sheep, and everyone is content. (Alternatively, a woman can come along, buy up the commons and start charging grazing fees. To ensure the longevity of her resource, she will naturally take care to avoid overgrazing.)

However, let us accept that under some circumstances the POTC is real, and cannot be overcome through the extension of private property rights. What solutions can then be brought to bear on the problem?

Solutions to social problems always fall into one of two categories: voluntary or coercive. Voluntary solutions to the POTC abound throughout history – the most notable being the kinds of social arrangements made by fishermen. When a number of fishing communities dot a lake, villagers develop complex and effective measures to ensure that the lake is not over-fished. Any display of wealth is frowned upon, since it is clear that wealth can only come from over-fishing. Communal leaders meet to figure out how much each village can catch – and it is very hard to hide your catch in a small village. Furthermore, the problem of not knowing exactly how much fish is being taken by others – as well as natural annual variations in fish stocks – lead to significant underestimation of allowable catches, which ensures that sustainability is always achieved. Left-leaning economists might be baffled by the POTC, but there is scant recorded historical evidence of illiterates in fishing villages regularly starving to death due to over-fishing (unless their village leaders were left-leaning economists perhaps).

The POTC is yet another manifestation of that old bugbear: the blind insistence that man is a being whose sole motivation is immediate financial considerations. (Economists who believe this and who also have children are most baffling in this regard!) "Ahhh," says the miserly farmer of this 'instant gratification' fairy tale, "I will graze my sheep by night and callously denude the commons, so I can grow a dozen extra turnips!" But what good will his extra turnips do him if no one in the village will talk to him, or when no one will help him build a barn, or when he gets sick and needs people to care for his sheep? No, even miserly farmers are far better obeying the rules and forgetting about their extra turnips – since they will lose far more than they gain by circumventing social norms. Communities have weapons of ostracism and contempt that *far* outweigh immediate economic calculations.

(Has this changed in the Internet age? Surely we are far less constrained by social norms than we used to be! Not at all – now, with tools ranging from credit reports, web searches and easy access to prior employers, conformity to basic decency is more important than ever.)

PROBLEM #2: THE STATE AS A 'COMMON'

However, let us assume that *none* of the above rebuttals to the POTC holds firm, and in certain circumstances there is simply no way to extend property rights to, or exercise social control over, resources which cannot be owned – what then? Do we turn such a thorny and complex problem to the tender mercies of the *State* to solve?

One of the most interesting aspects of using the State to solve the POTC *is that the State **itself** is subject to the problem of the commons.*

Since the State is an entity wherein property is owned in "common," the problem of selfish exploitation leading to general destruction applies as surely to State "property" as it does to the common land ringed by greedy and short-sighted farmers. Just as farmers can destroy the commons while pursuing their individual self-interest, so can politicians, bureaucrats, lobbyists and other assorted State toadies and courtiers destroy the economy *as a whole* in pursuit of their own selfish economic and political goals.

The POTC argues that, due to "common ownership," long-term prosperity is sacrificed for the sake of short-term advantage. Because no one defends and maintains property that can be utilized by all, that property is pillaged into oblivion. And – the *State* is supposed to solve this problem? How? That is *exactly* how the State operates!

Let's look at some examples of how the State pillages the future for the sake of greed in the here-and-now:

- deficit financing;
- inflationary monetary expansion;
- government bonds, which future generations must pay out;
- spending the money taken in through social security, which future generations must pay for;
- offensive "defense" spending, which future citizens will pay for through increased risk of domestic attacks;
- massive educational failures, which have immensely deleterious effects on future productivity and happiness;
- the granting of special powers, rights and benefits to lobbyists such as unions, public sector employees and large corporations, which results in higher prices and deficits (the cost to the US economy for union laws alone is calculated at $50 *trillion* dollars over the past 50 years);
- the failure to adequately maintain public infrastructure such as roads, schools, bridges, the water supply and so on, which passes enormous liabilities onto the next generation;
- massive spending on the war on drugs, which increases crime in the future;
- the pollution of public lands and other fixed assets, which saves money in the short run while ruining value in the long run;
- ...and goodness knows how much more!

From the above examples, it is easy to see that the POTC applies to the State to a far greater degree than any other social agency or individual. If we recall our group of greedy farmers, we can easily see that they have a strong incentive to avoid or solve the POTC, since it is they *themselves* who will suffer from the despoiling of un-owned lands. However, in the case of the State, those who prey upon and despoil the public purse will *never themselves face the direct consequences of their pillaging*. Thus their incentive to prevent, solve or even alleviate the problem is virtually non-existent.

Furthermore, even if the farmers do end up destroying the un-owned lands, they can at least get together and voluntarily work to find a better solution in the future. Once the government takes over a problem, however, control passes almost completely from the private sphere to the public sphere of enforcement, corruption and politics. Once firmly planted in the realm of the State, not only is the problem of public ownership made incalculably worse, but it cannot ever be resolved, since the predation of the public purse is now defended by all the armed might of the State military. Consequences evaporate, competition is eliminated, and a mad free-for-all grab-fest simply escalates until the public purse is drained dry and the State collapses. (This is what happened in the Soviet Union; in the 1980s, as it became clear that communism was unsustainable, Kremlin insiders simply pillaged the public treasury until the State went bankrupt.)

Thus the idea of turning to the State to solve the POTC is akin to the old medical joke about the operation being a complete success, with the minor exception that the patient died. If the POTC *is* a significant issue in the private sector, then turning it over to the government makes it staggeringly worse – turning it from a mildly challenging problem of economics into a suicidal expansion of State power and violence. If the problem of the commons is *not* a significant issue, then surely we do not need the State to solve it at all.

Either way, there is no compelling evidence or argument to be made for the value, morality or efficacy of turning problems of public ownership over to the armed might of the State. Both logically and ethically, it is the equivalent of treating a mild headache with a guillotine.

If the State is an evil, corrupt and destructive solution to the problems of social organization, what alternatives can anarchism offer?

Dispute Resolution Organizations

An essential aspect of economic life is the ability to enforce contracts and resolve intractable disputes. How can a stateless society provide these functions in the absence of a government?

The first thing to understand about contracts is that they are a form of insurance, insofar as they attempt to minimize the risks of noncompliance. If I enter into a five-year mortgage agreement with a bank, I will attempt to minimize my risks by requiring that the bank give me a fixed interest rate for the time period of the contract. My bank, on the other hand, will minimize its risk by retaining ownership of my house as collateral, in case I do not pay the mortgage.

In a world without risk, contracts would be unnecessary, and everyone would do business on a handshake. However, there are people who are dishonest, scatter-brained, manipulative and false, and so we need contracts which basically spell out the penalties for noncompliance to particular requirements.

In modern statist societies, contracts are generally enforced not through the court system, but rather through the *threat* of the court system. I was in business for many years, at an executive level, and I never once heard of a contract being success-fully enforced through the state court system, although I did on occasion hear litigious threats – which is quite different. The threat was not so much, "I am going to use the court to enforce this contract," but rather, "I am going to use the threat of *taking* you to court in order to enforce this contract." The prospect of expensive and time-con-suming legal action was always enough to force a resolution of some kind. No *actual* court compulsion was ever required.

It is quite easy to see that when a process that is designed to mediate disputes becomes itself a threat which causes disputes to be mediated privately, it has largely failed in its intent. State court systems have become like the quasi-private car insur-ance companies – the threats and inconvenience of using them has caused most peo-ple to settle their disputes privately, rather than involve themselves in something that they are forced to pay for, but can almost never use.

This bodes very well for anarchic solutions to contract disputes.

In a stateless society, entrepreneurs will be very willing and eager to provide cre-ative solutions to the problems of contractual noncompliance. As a nonviolent solu-tion, the profits will be maximized if noncompliance can be *prevented*, rather than merely addressed after the fact.

To take a simple example, let us pretend that you are a loans officer at a bank, and I come in requesting $10,000. Naturally, you will be very happy to lend me the money if I will pay back both the principal and interest on time, since that is how you make your profit. However, such a guarantee is completely impossible, since even if I have the money and the intent to pay you back, I could get hit by a bus while on my way to do so, leaving you perhaps $10,000 in the hole.

What questions will you need to answer in order to assess the risk? You will want to know two things in particular:

1. Have I consistently paid back loans in the past?
2. Do I have any collateral for the loan?

These two pieces of information are somewhat related. If I have consistently paid back loans in the past, then your need for collateral will be diminished. The more collateral that I am able to provide for the loan, the less it is necessary for me to have a good credit history.

The reason that a good credit history is so necessary is not just to establish my credit worthiness, but also to help the bank assess how much I have currently invested into my good reputation. If I have taken out loans for hundreds of thousands of dollars in the past, and repaid them on time, then it scarcely seems likely that I would have gone through all of that just to steal $10,000.

If we say that my good credit rating saves me two percentage points on my interest payments, and that I will need a further $500,000 of loans over the course of my life, then my good credit rating will be saving me at a bare minimum tens of thousands of dollars. Thus, I would end up *losing* money if I took out a $10,000 loan and did not pay it back, since the cash benefit would not cover the losses I would incur through the destruction of my credit rating. Physical "collateral" is thus less required, since I have the very real "collateral" of a good credit rating.

These kinds of economic calculations occur regularly in a statist society, and would not vanish like the morning mist in a stateless society.

However, there are certain kinds of loans that some financial institutions would be willing to make, despite the high level of risk involved. Young people just starting out – who have no family to provide collateral – would be in a higher risk category, as would those who had failed to make loan payments in the past. As we can see from late-night television commercials for cars, no credit history – or even a bad credit history – does not make one permanently ineligible for loans.

There are two main ways to manage risk in any complex situation – *hedging*, and *insurance*. The "hedging" approach is to bet both *for* and *against* a particular outcome. In the world of currency trading, this means betting a certain amount that the dollar will go up, and another amount that the dollar will go down. In the world of horse racing, it means betting on more than one horse. This is also why people diversify their stock portfolios.

The "insurance" approach tends to be used where hedging is impossible. When I was an executive in the software world, my employees would often take out insurance in case I got sick or died. It was relatively impossible to "hedge" this risk, because keeping "backup employees" in a basement is not particularly cost-efficient, let alone moral. Life insurance is another example of this.

These strategies are already well-established in the current quasi-free market. However, in one-to-one contracts, state courts retain their monopoly. If I am an employee, I have a one-to-one contract with my employer; I cannot "hedge" the risks involved in this contract, and currently neither can I buy insurance to mitigate the risk that my employer will go out of business, while still owing me pay and expenses.

In the absence of a government, the need for the rational mitigation of risk in contracts would still be there, and entrepreneurs will inevitably provide creative and intelligent solutions to address this.

BREAKING CONTRACT

Let us take a relatively small example of how contract disputes can be resolved in a stateless society.

Let us say that I pay you $15,000 to landscape my garden, but you never show up to do the work. Ideally, I would like my $15,000 back, as well as another few thousand dollars for my inconvenience. In a stateless society, when we first put pen to paper on a contract, we can choose an impartial third party to mediate any dispute. If a conflict should arise that we cannot solve ourselves, we contractually agree in advance to abide by the decision of this Dispute Resolution Organization (DRO).

Since I am not an expert in pursuing people and getting money from them, if I had any doubts about your motives, capacity and honesty, I would simply pay this DRO a fee to recompense me if the deal goes awry. If you run off without doing the work, I simply submit my claim to the DRO, who then pays me $20,000.

When I first apply for this insurance, the DRO will charge me a certain amount of money, based on their evaluation of the risk I am taking by doing business with you. If you have cheated your last ten customers, the DRO will simply not insure the contract, thus implicitly informing me of the risk that I am taking. If you have a spotty record, then the DRO may charge me a few thousand dollars to insure your work – again, giving me a pretty good sense of how reliable you are.

On the other hand, if you have been in business for 30 years, and have never once cheated a customer, or received a complaint, then the DRO is simply insuring against delays caused by sudden madness or unexpected death. It may only charge me $50 for this eventuality.

This form of contract insurance is a very powerful positive incentive for honest dealings in business. The cost of insuring a contract is directly added to the cost of doing business, and so if it can be kept as low as humanly possible, the financial benefits to both parties are clear.

The cost of insuring a contract can be kept even lower if you are willing to provide collateral upfront. What this means is that if you cheat me out of the $15,000, and the DRO has to pay me $20,000, you promise to pay the DRO $25,000. If you cheat me, the DRO can then take this money directly out of your bank account.

In this way, contracts can be enforced without resorting to violence, or lengthy and incredibly expensive court battles. The risks of entering into contracts are clearly communicated up front, and honest people will be directly rewarded through lower enforcement costs, just as non-smokers are directly rewarded through lower life insurance costs.

Non-Payment

Suppose I have contracted with a DRO to pay restitution if I cannot fulfill my business obligations in some way, and end up owing them $100,000. What happens if I cannot pay, or simply refuse to pay?

Currently, the State will use violence against me if I do not pay. While this may be a satisfying form of medieval vengeance gratification, it scarcely helps me cough up $100,000 that the DRO actually wants from me. In a stateless society, what options are available for the DRO to get its money?

In any modern economy, individuals are bound by dozens of obligations and contracts, from apartment leases to gym memberships to credit cards contracts to insurance agreements. The costs of doing business with people who are known to honor their contracts is far lower, which is why it seems highly likely that a stateless society produce both DROs, and Contract Rating Agencies (CRAs).

CRAs would be independent entities that would objectively evaluate an individual's contract compliance. If I become known as a man who regularly breaks his contracts, it will become more and more difficult for me to efficiently operate in a complex economy. This form of economic ostracism is an immensely powerful – and nonviolent – tool for promoting compliance to social norms and moral rules.

If an individual egregiously violates social norms – and we shall get to the issue of violent crime below – then one incredibly effective option that society has is to *simply cease doing any form of business with such an individual.*

If I cheat my DRO – or another individual – out of an enormous sum of money, the CRA could simply revoke my contract rating completely.

DROs would very likely have provisions which would simply state that they would not enforce any contract with anyone whose contract rating was revoked. In other words, if I run a hotel, and an "outcast" wants to rent a room, I will be immediately aware of this, since I will enter his credit card, and be promptly informed that no contract will be honored with this individual. In other words, if he sets fire to my hotel, steals or destroys property, or harasses another guest, then my DRO will not help me at all. Will I be likely to want to rent a room to this fellow, or will I tell him that, sadly, the hotel is full?

In the same way, grocery stores, taxicabs, bus companies, electricity providers, banks, restaurants and other such organizations will be very unlikely to want to do business with such an outcast, since they will have no protection if he misbehaves.

Economic interactions, of course, are purely voluntary, and no man can be morally forced to do business with another man. People who cheat and steal and lie will be highly visible in a stateless society, and will find that other people will turn away from them more often than not, unless they change their ways, and provide restitution for their prior wrongs.

An outcast can get his contract rating restored if he is willing to repay those he has wronged. If he gets a job and allows his wages to be garnished until his debts are paid off, his contract rating can be restored, at least to the minimum level required for him to hold a job and rent an apartment. A DRO, which is always interested in preventing recurrence, rather than dealing with consequences, may also reduce his burden if he is willing to attend psychological and credit counseling education.

In this way, contracts can be enforced without resorting to violence – the tool of economic and social ostracism is the most powerful method for dealing with those who repeatedly violate moral and social rules. We do not need to throw people into economically unproductive "debtor's prisons" or send men with guns to kidnap and incarcerate them – all we need to do is publish their crimes for all to see, and let the natural justice of society take care of the rest.

Ah, but what if an "outcast" has been treated unjustly, and is being blackmailed by a DRO or CRA?

Well, remember that anarchism is always a *two-sided* negotiation. In order to get people to sign up to your DRO or CRA, what checks and balances would you put in your contracts to calm their fears in this regard?

THE STATELESS SOCIETY: AN EXAMINATION OF ALTERNATIVES

Let us turn to a more detailed examination of how private agencies could work in a free society.

Remember, these are only possible ideas about how such agencies could work – I'm sure that you have many of your own, which may be vastly superior to mine. The purpose of this section is not to create some sort of finalized blueprint for a stateless society, but to show how the various incentives and methodologies of freedom can create powerful and productive solutions to complex social problems, in a way that will forever elude a statist society.

We will start with a few articles that I originally published in 2005, which go over my theory of Dispute Resolution Organizations – DROs. More details about this approach are available in my podcast series as well.

If the Twentieth Century proved anything, it is that the single greatest danger to human life is the centralized political State, which murdered more than 200 million souls. Modern States are the last and greatest remaining predators. It is clear that the danger has not abated with the demise of communism and fascism. All Western democracies currently face vast and accelerating escalations of State power and centralized control over economic and civic life. In almost all Western democracies, the State chooses:

- where children go to school, and how they will be educated;
- the interest rate citizens can borrow at;
- the value of currency;
- how employees can be hired and fired;
- how more than 50% of their citizen's time and money are disposed of;
- who a citizen may choose as a doctor;
- what kinds of medical procedures can be received – and when;
- when to go to war;
- who can live in the country;
- ...just to touch on a few.

Most of these amazing intrusions into personal liberty have occurred over the past 90 years, since the introduction of the income tax. They have been accepted by a population helpless to challenge the expansion of State power – and yet, even though most citizens have received endless pro-State propaganda in government schools, a growing rebellion is brewing. The endless and increasing State predations are now so intrusive that they have effectively arrested the forward momentum of society, which now hangs before a fall. Children are poorly educated, young people are unable to get ahead, couples with children fall ever-further into debt, and the elderly are finding their medical systems collapsing under the weight of their growing needs. And none of this takes into account the ever-growing State debts.

These early years of the twenty-first century are thus the end of an era, a collapse of mythology comparable to the fall of communism, monarchy, or political Christianity. The idea that the State is even *capable* of solving social problems is now viewed with great skepticism – which foretells the imminent end, since as soon as skepticism is applied to the State, the State falls, since it fails at everything except expansion, and so can only survive on propaganda.

Yet while most people are comfortable with the *idea* of reducing the size and power of the State, they become distinctly uncomfortable with the idea of getting rid of it completely. To use a medical analogy, if the State is a cancer, they prefer medicating it into remission, rather than eliminating it completely.

This can never work. If history has proven anything, it is the simple fact that States always expand until they destroy society. Because the State uses violence to achieve its ends, and there is no rational end to the expansion of violence, States grow until they destroy the host civilization through the corruption of money, contracts, civility and liberty. As such, the cancerous metaphor is not misplaced. People who believe that the State can somehow be contained have not accepted the fact that no State in history has ever been contained.

Even the rare reductions are merely temporary. The United States was founded on the principle of limited government; it took little more than a few decades for the State to break the bonds of the Constitution, implement the income tax, take control the money supply, and begin its catastrophic expansion. There is no example in history of a State being permanently reduced in size. All that happens during a tax or civil revolt is that the State retrenches, figures out what it did wrong, and begins its expansion again – or provokes a war, which silences all but fringe dissenters.

Given these well-known historical facts, why do people continue believe that such a deadly predator can be tamed? Surely it can only be because they consider a slow strangulation in the grip of an expanding State somehow better than the "quick death" of a society bereft of a State.

Why do most people believe that a coercive and monopolistic social agency is required for society to function? There are a number of answers to this question, but they tend to revolve around four central points:

1. Dispute resolution;
2. Collective services;
3. Pollution, and;
4. Crime.

We will tackle the first three in this section, and the last one in the next.

Dispute Resolution

It is quite amazing that people still believe that the State somehow facilitates the resolution of disputes, given the fact that modern courts are out of the reach of all but the most wealthy and patient. In my experience, to take a dispute with a stockbroker to the court system would have cost more than a quarter of a million dollars and from five to ten years – however, a private mediator settled the matter within a few months for very little money. In the realm of marital dissolution, private mediators are commonplace. Unions use grievance processes, and a plethora of specialists in dispute resolution have sprung up to fill in the void left by a ridiculously lengthy, expensive and incompetent State court system.

Thus it cannot be that people actually believe that the State is required for dispute resolution, since the court apparatus is unavailable to the vast majority of the population, who resolve their disputes either privately or through agreed-upon mediators.

Collective Services

Roads, sewage, water and electricity and so on are all cited as reasons why a State must exist. How roads could be privately paid for remains such an impenetrable mystery that most people are willing to support the State – and so ensure the continual undermining of civil society – rather than concede that this problem is solvable. There are many ways to pay for roads, such as electronic or cash tolls, GPS charges, roads maintained by the businesses they lead to, or communal organizations and so on. The problem that a water company might build plumbing to a community, and then charge exorbitant fees for supplying it, is equally easy to counter, as mentioned above.

None of these problems touch the central rationale for a State. They are all *ex post facto* justifications made to avoid the need for critical examination or, heaven forbid, a support of anarchism.

It is completely contradictory to argue that voluntary free-market relations are "bad" – and that the only way to combat them is to impose a compulsory monopoly on the market. If voluntary interactions are bad, how can coercive monopolies be better?

State provision of public services inevitably leads to the following:

- The granting of favorable contracts to political allies;
- Tax-subsidized costs leading to over-use, and intergenerational debt;
- A lack of renewal investment in infrastructure leading to expensive deterioration;
- A growth in coercive pro-union legislation, which spreads inefficiencies to other industries;
- A lack of innovation and exploration of alternatives to existing systems of production and distribution, and;
- A dangerous social dependence on a single provider.

…and many more such inefficiencies, problems and predations.

Due to countless examples of free market solutions to the problem of "carrier costs," this argument no longer holds the kind of water is used to, so people must turn elsewhere to justify the continued existence of the State.

POLLUTION

This is perhaps the greatest problem faced by free market theorists. It is worth spending a little time on outlining the worst possible scenario, to see how a voluntary system could solve it. However, it is important to first dispel the notion that the State currently deals effectively with pollution. Firstly, the most polluted land on the planet is State-owned, because States do not profit from retaining the value of their property. Secondly, the distribution of mineral, lumber and drilling rights is directly skewed towards bribery and corruption, because States never sell the land, but rather just the resource rights. A lumber company cannot buy woodlands from the State, just harvesting rights. Thus the State gets a renewable source of income, and can further coerce lumber companies by enforcing re-seeding. This, of course, tends to promote bribery, corruption and the creation of "fly-by-night" lumber companies which strip the land bare, but vanish when it comes time to re-seed. Selling State land to a private company easily solves this problem, because a company that was willing to re-seed would reap the greatest long-term profits from the woodland, and therefore would be able to bid the most for the land.

Also, it should be remembered that, in the realm of air pollution, States created the problem in the first place. In England, when industrial smokestacks first began belching fumes into the orchards of apple farmers, the farmers took the factory-owners to court, citing the common-law tradition of restitution for property damage. Sadly, however, the capitalists had gotten to the State courts first, and had more money to bribe with, employed more voting workers, and contributed more tax revenue than the farmers – and so the farmer's cases were thrown out of court. The judge argued that the "common good" of the factories trumped the "private need" of the farmers. The free market did not *fail* to solve the problem of air pollution – it was forcibly *prevented* from doing so because the State was corrupted.

However, it is a sticking point, so it is worth examining in detail how the free market might solve the problem of air pollution. One egregious example often cited is a group of houses downwind from a new factory which is busy night and day coating them in soot.

Now, when a man buys a new house, isn't it important to him to ensure that he will not be coated with someone else's refuse? The need for a clean and safe environment is so strong that it is a clear invitation for enterprising entrepreneurs to sweat bullets figuring out how to provide it.

If a group of homeowners is afraid of pollution, the first thing they will do is buy *pollution insurance*, which is a natural response to a situation where costs cannot be predicted but consequences are dire.

Let us say that a homeowner named John buys pollution insurance which pays him two million dollars if the air in or around his house becomes polluted. In other words, as long as John's air remains clean, his insurance company makes money.

One day, a plot of land up-wind of John's house comes up for sale. Naturally, his insurance company would be very interested in this, and would monitor the sale. If the purchaser is some private school, all is well (assuming John has not bought noise pollution insurance). If, however, the insurance company discovers that Sally's House of Polluting Paint Production is interested in purchasing the plot of land, it will likely spring into action, taking one of the following courses:

* Buying the land itself, then selling it to a non-polluting buyer;
* Getting assurances from Sally that her company will not pollute;
* Paying Sally to enter into a non-polluting contract.

If, however, someone at the insurance company is asleep at the wheel, and Sally buys the land and puts up her polluting factory, what happens then?

Well, then the insurance company is on the hook for $2M to John (assuming for the moment that only John bought pollution insurance). Thus, it can afford to pay Sally up to $2M to reduce her pollution and still be cash-positive. This payment could take many forms, from the installation of pollution-control equipment to a buy-out to a subsidy for under-production and so on.

If the $2M is not enough to solve the problem, then the insurance company pays John the $2M and he goes and buys a new house in an unpolluted neighbourhood. However, this scenario is highly unlikely, since the insurance company would be unlikely to insure only one single person in a neighbourhood against air pollution.

So, that is the view from John's air-pollution insurance company. What about the view from Sally's House of Polluting Paint Production? She, also, must be covered by a DRO in order to buy land, borrow money and hire employees. How does that DRO view her tendency to pollute?

Pollution brings damage claims against Sally, because pollution is by definition damage to persons or property. Thus Sally's DRO would take a dim view of her pollution, since it would be on the hook for any damage her factory causes. In fact, it would be most unlikely that Sally's DRO would insure her against damages unless she were able to prove that she would be able to operate her factory without harming the property of those around her. And without a DRO, of course, she would be unable to start her factory, borrow money, hire employees etc.

It is important to remember that DROs, much like cell phone companies, only prosper if they cooperate. Sally's DRO only makes money if Sally does not pollute. John's insurer also only makes money if Sally does not pollute. Thus the two companies share a common goal, which fosters cooperation.

Finally, even if John is not insured against air pollution, he can use his and/or Sally's DRO to gain restitution for the damage her pollution is causing to his property. Both Sally and John's DROs would have reciprocity agreements, since John wants to be protected against Sally's actions, and Sally wants to be protected against John's actions. Because of this desire for mutual protection, they would choose DROs which had the widest reciprocity agreements.

Thus, in a truly free market, there are many levels and agencies actively working against pollution. John's insurer will be actively scanning the surroundings looking for polluters it can forestall. Sally will be unable to build her paint factory without proving that she will not pollute. Mutual or independent DROs will resolve any disputes regarding property damage caused by Sally's pollution.

There are other benefits as well, which are almost unsolvable in the current system. Imagine that Sally's smokestacks are so high that her air pollution sails over John's house and lands on Reginald's house, a hundred miles away. Reginald then complains to his DRO/insurer that his property is being damaged. His DRO will examine the air contents and wind currents, then trace the pollution back to its source and resolve the dispute with Sally's DRO. If the air pollution is particularly complicated, then Reginald's DRO will place non-volatile compounds into Sally's smokestacks and follow them to where they land. This can be used in a situation where a number of different factories may be contributing pollutants.

The problem of inter-country air pollution may seem to be a sticky one, but it is easily solvable – even if we accept that countries will still exist. Obviously, a Canadian living along the Canada/US border, for instance, will not choose a DRO which refuses to cover air pollution emanating from the US. Thus the DRO will have to have reciprocity agreements with the DROs across the border. If the US DROs refuse to have reciprocity agreements with the Canadian DROs – inconceivable, since the pollution can go both ways – then the Canadian DRO will simply start a US branch and compete.

The difference is that international DROs actually profit from cooperation, in a way that governments do not. For instance, a State government on the Canada/US border has little motivation to impose pollution costs on local factories, as long as the pollution generally goes north. For DRO's, quite the opposite would be true.

There are so many benefits to the concept of State-less DRO's that they could easily fill volumes. A few can be touched on here, to further highlight the value of the idea.

In a condominium building, ownership is conditional upon certain rules. Even though a man "owns" the property, he cannot throw all-night parties, or keep five large dogs, or operate a brothel. Without the coercive blanket of a central State, the opportunities for a wide variety of communities arise, which will largely eliminate the current social conflicts about the direction of society as a whole.

For instance, some people like guns to be available, while others prefer them to be unavailable. Currently, a battle rages for control of the State so that one group can enforce its will on the other. That's unnecessary. With DRO's, communities can be formed in which guns are either permitted, or not permitted. Marijuana can be approved or forbidden. Half your income can be deducted for various social schemes, or you can keep it all for yourself. Sunday shopping can be allowed, or disallowed. It is completely up to the individual to choose what kind of society he or she wants to live in. The ownership of property in such communities is conditional on following certain rules, and if those rules prove onerous or unpleasant, the owner can sell and move at any time. Another plus is that all these "societies" exist as little laboratories, and can prove or disprove various theories about gun ownership, drug legalization and so on, thus contributing to people's knowledge about the best rules for communities.

One or two problems exist, however, which cannot be spirited away. A person who decides to live "off the grid" – or exist without any DRO representation – can theoretically get away with a lot. However, that is also true in the existing statist system. If a man currently decides to become homeless, he can more or less commit crimes at will – but he also gives up all beneficial and enforceable forms of social cooperation. Thus although DROs may not solve the problem of utter lawlessness, neither does the current system, so all is equal.

Interpersonal Crimes

Crimes against persons, such as murder and rape, are generally considered separate and distinct from those against property. However, this is a fairly modern distinction. In the European system of common law, crimes against persons were often punished through the confiscation of property. A rape cost the rapist such-and-such amount, a murder five times as much, and so on. This sort of arrangement is generally preferred by victims, who currently not only suffer from physical violation – but must also pay taxes to incarcerate the criminal. A woman who is raped would usually rather receive a quarter of a million dollars than pay a thousand dollars annually to cage her rapist, which adds insult to injury. Thus, crimes against persons and crimes against property are not as distinct as they may seem, since both commonly require property as restitution. A man who rapes a woman, then, incurs a debt to her of some hundreds of thousands of dollars, and must pay it or be ejected from all the economic benefits of society.

Finally, one other advantage can be termed the "Scrabble-Challenge Benefit." In Scrabble, an accuser loses his turn if he challenges another player's word and the challenge fails. Given the costs of resolving disputes, DROs would be very careful to ensure that those bringing false accusations would be punished through their own premiums, their contract ratings and by also assuming the entire cost of the dispute. This would greatly reduce the number of frivolous lawsuits, to the great benefit of all.

On a personal note, it has been my experience that, in talking over these matters for the last twenty-odd years, people honestly claim that they cannot conceive of a society without a centralized and coercive State. To which I feel compelled to ask them: exactly how many lawsuits have you pursued in your own life? I have yet to find even one person who has prosecuted a lawsuit through to conclusion. I also ask them whether they maintain their jobs through threats or blackmail. None. Do they keep their spouses chained in the basement? Not a one. Are their friends forced to spend time with them? Do they steal from the grocery store? Nope.

In other words, I say, it is clear that, although you say that you cannot imagine a society without a coercive State, you have only to look in the mirror to see how such a world might work. Everyone who is in your life is there by choice. Everyone you deal with on a personal or professional relationship interacts with you on a voluntary basis. You don't use violence in your own life at all. If you are unsatisfied with a product, you return it. If you stop desiring a lover, you part. If you dislike a job, you quit. You force no one – and yet you say that society cannot exist without force. It is very hard to understand. People then reply that they do not need to use coercion because the State is there to protect them. I then ask them if they know how impossible it is to actually *use* the court system. They agree, of course, because they know it takes many years and a small fortune to approach even the vague possibility of justice. I also ask them if they are themselves burning to knock over an old woman and snatch her purse, but fear the police too greatly. Of course not. They just think that everyone else is. Well, after twenty years of conversations, I can tell you all: it's not the case. Most people, given the correct incentives, act entirely honourably.

Of course, evil people exist. There are cold, sociopathic monsters in our midst. It is precisely because of the human capacity for evil that a centralized State always undermines society. Due to our capacity for sadism, our only hope is to decentralize authority, so that the evil among us can never rise to a station greater than that of excluded, hunted criminals. To create a State and give it the power of life and death does not solve the problem of human evil. It merely transforms the shallow desire for easy property to the bottomless lust for political power.

The idea that society can – and must – exist without a centralized State is the greatest lesson that the grisly years of the Twentieth Century can teach us. Our own society cannot escape the general doom of history, the inevitable destiny of social collapse as the State eats its own inhabitants. Our choice is not between the State and the free market, but between death and life. Whatever the risks of dissolving the central State, they are far less than the certain destruction of allowing it to escalate, as it inevitably will. Like a cancer patient facing certain demise, we must reach for whatever medicine shows the most promise, and not wait until it is too late.

The Stateless Society and Violent Crime

You might well now be thinking: how can a stateless society deal with violent criminals?

This challenging question can be answered using three approaches. The first is to examine how such criminals are dealt with at present; the second is to divide violent crimes into crimes of *motive* and crimes of *passion*, and the third is to show how a stateless society would deal with both categories of crime far better than any existing system.

The first question is: how are violent criminals dealt with at present? The honest answer, to any unbiased observer, is surely: *they are encouraged.*

A basic fact of life is that people respond to incentives. The better that crime pays, the more people will become criminals. Certain well-known habits – drugs, gambling, and prostitution in particular – are non-violent in nature, but highly desired by certain segments of the population. If these non-violent behaviors are criminalized, the profit gained by providing these services rises. Criminalizing voluntary interactions destroys all stabilizing social forces (contracts, open activity, knowledge-sharing and mediation), and so violence becomes the norm for dispute resolution.

Furthermore, wherever a law creates an environment where most criminals make more money than the police, the police simply become bribed into compliance. By increasing the profits of non-violent activities, the State ensures the corruption of the police and judicial system – thus making it both safer and more profitable to operate outside the law. It can take dozens of arrests to actually face trial – and many trials to gain a conviction. Policemen now spend about a third of their time filling out paperwork – and 90% of their time chasing non-violent criminals. Entire sections of certain cities are run by gangs of thugs, and the jails are overflowing with harmless low-level peons sent to jail as make-work for the judicial system – thus constantly increasing law-enforcement costs. Peaceful citizens are also legally disarmed through gun control laws. In this manner, the modern State literally creates, protects and profits from violent criminals.

Thus the standard to compare the stateless society's response to violent crime is not some perfect world where thugs are effectively dealt with, but rather the current mess where violence is both encouraged and protected.

Before we turn to how a stateless society deals with crime, however, it is essential to remember that the stateless society automatically eliminates the greatest violence faced by almost all of us – the State that threatens us with guns if we don't hand over our money – and our lives, should it decide to declare war. Thus it cannot be said that the existing system is one which minimizes violence. Quite the contrary – the honest population is violently enslaved by the State, and the dishonest provided with cash incentives and protection.

State violence – in its many forms – has been growing in Western societies over the past fifty years, as regulation, tariffs and taxation have all risen exponentially. National debts are an obvious form of intergenerational theft. Support of foreign governments also increases violence, since these governments use subsidies to buy arms and further terrorize their own populations. The arms market is also funded and controlled by governments. The list of State crimes can go on and on, but one last gulag is worth mentioning – all the millions of poor souls kidnapped and held hostage in prisons for non-violent "crimes."

Since existing States terrorize, enslave and incarcerate literally *billions* of citizens, it is hard to understand how they can be seen as effectively working *against* violence in any form.

How does a stateless society deal with violence? First, it is important to differentiate the use of force into crimes of *motive* and crimes of *passion*. Crimes of *motive* are open to correction through changing incentives; any system which reduces the profits of property crimes – while increasing the profits of honest labor – will reduce these crimes. In the last part of this section, we will see how the stateless society achieves this better than any other option.

Crimes of motive can be diminished by making crime a low-profit activity relative to working for a living. Crime entails labor, and if most people could make more money working honestly for the same amount of labor, there will be far fewer criminals.

As you have read above, in a stateless society, Dispute Resolution Organizations (DROs) flourish through the creation of voluntary contracts between interested parties, and all property is private. How does this affect violent crime?

Let's look at "break and enter." If I own a house, I will probably take out insurance against theft. Obviously, my insurance company benefits most from *preventing* theft, and so will encourage me to get an alarm system and so on, just as occurs now.

This situation is more or less analogous to what happens now – with the not-inconsequential adjustment that, since DROs handle *policing* as well as *restitution*, their motives for preventing theft or rendering stolen property useless is far higher than it is now. As such, much more investment in prevention would be worthwhile, such as creating "voice activated" appliances which only work for their owners.

However, the stateless society goes much, much further in preventing crime – specifically, by *identifying those who are going to become criminals, and preventing that transition*. In this situation, the stateless society is far more effective than any State system.

In a stateless society, contracts with DROs are required to maintain any sort of economic life – without DRO representation, citizens are unable to get a job, hire employees, rent a car, buy a house or send their children to school. Any DRO will naturally ensure that its contracts include penalties for violent crimes – so if you steal a car, your DRO has the right to use force or ostracism against you to get the car back – and probably retrieve financial penalties to boot.

How does this work in practice? Let's take a test case. Say that you wake up one morning and decide to become a thief. Well, the first thing you have to do is cancel your coverage with your DRO, so that your DRO has less incentive against you when you steal, since you are no longer a customer. DROs would have clauses allowing you to cancel your coverage, just as insurance companies have now. Thus you would have to notify your DRO that you were dropping coverage. No problem, you're off their list.

However, DROs as a *whole* really need to keep track of people who have opted out of the entire DRO system, since those people have clearly signaled their intention to go rogue and live "off the grid." Thus if you cancel your DRO insurance, your name goes into a database available to all DROs. If you sign up with another DRO, no problem, your name is taken out. However, if you do not sign up with *any other* DRO, red flags pop up all over the system.

What happens then? Remember – there is no public property in a stateless society. If you've gone rogue, where are you going to go? You can't take a bus – bus companies will not take rogues, because *their* DRO will require that they take only DRO-covered passengers, in case of injury or altercation. Want to fill up on gas? No luck, for the same reason. You can try hitchhiking, of course, which might work, but what happens when you get to your destination and try to rent a motel room? No DRO card, no luck. Want to sleep in the park? Parks are privately owned, so keep moving. Getting hungry? No groceries, no restaurants – no food! What are you going to do?

So, really, what incentive is there to turn to a life of crime? Working for a living – and being protected by a DRO – pays really well. Going off the grid and becoming a rogue pits the entire weight of the combined DRO system against you – and, even if you *do* manage to survive and steal something, it has probably been voice-encoded or protected in some other manner against unauthorized use.

Let's suppose that you somehow bypass all of *that*, and do manage to steal, where are you going to sell your stolen goods? You're not protected by a DRO, so who will buy from you, knowing they have no recourse if something goes wrong? And besides, anyone who interacts with you may be dropped from the DRO system too, and face all the attendant difficulties.

Will there be underground markets? Perhaps – but where would they operate? People need a place to live, cars to rent, clothes to buy, groceries to eat. No DRO means no participation in economic life.

As well, prostitution, gambling and drugs will not be "illegal" in a stateless society – and the elimination of the war on drugs alone would, it has been estimated, eliminate 80% of violent crime. There are no import duties or restrictions, so smuggling becomes completely pointless. Currency would be private, as we will see below, so counterfeiting will be much harder.

Plus, no taxation – the take-home pay for an honest worker is *far* higher in a stateless society!

Fewer opportunities, lower profits – and greater incentives to do an honest day's work – there is no better way to steer those who respond to incentives alone away from a life of crime.

Thus it is fair to say that any stateless society will do a far better job of protecting its citizens against crimes of motive – what, then, about crimes of passion?

Crimes of Passion

Crimes of passion are harder to prevent – but also present far less of a threat to those outside of the circle in which they occur.

Let's say that a man kills his wife. They are both covered by DROs, of course, and their DRO contracts would include specific prohibitions against murder. Thus, the man would be subject to all the sanctions involved in his contract – probably confined labor and rehabilitation until a certain financial penalty was paid off, since DROs would be responsible for paying such penalties to any next of kin.

Fine, you say, but what if either the man or woman was not covered by a DRO? Well, where would they live? No one would rent them an apartment. If they own their house free and clear, who would sell them food? Or gas, water or electricity? Who would employ them? What bank would accept their money?

Let's say that only the murderous husband – planning to kill his wife – opted out of his DRO system without telling her. The first thing that his wife's DRO would do is inform her of her husband's action – and the ill intent it may represent – and help her relocate if desired. If she decided against relocation, her DRO would promptly drop her, since by deciding to live in close proximity with a rogue man, she was exposing herself to an untenable amount of danger (and so the DRO to a high risk for financial loss). Now, both the husband and wife have chosen to live without DROs, in a state of nature, and thus face all the insurmountable problems of getting food, shelter, money and so on.

Thus, murderers would be subject to the punishments of their DRO restrictions, or would signal their intent by dropping DRO coverage beforehand, when intervention would be possible.

Let's look at something slightly more complicated – stalking. A woman becomes obsessed with a man, and starts calling him at all hours and following him around.

Perhaps boils a bunny or two. If the man has bought insurance against stalking, his DRO will leap into action. It will call the woman's DRO, which then says to her: stop stalking this man or we'll drop you. And how does *her* DRO know whether she has really given up her stalking? Well, the man stops reporting it. And if there is a dispute, she just wears an ankle bracelet for a while to make sure. And remember – since there is no public property, she can be ordered off sidewalks, streets and parks.

(If the man has not bought insurance against stalking, no problem – it will just be more expensive to buy with a "pre-existing condition.")

Although they may seem unfamiliar to you, DROs are not a new concept – they are as ancient as civilization itself, but have been shouldered aside by the constant escalation of State power over the last century or so. In the past, undesired social behaviour was punished through ostracism, and risks ameliorated through voluntary "friendly societies." A man who left his wife and children – or a woman who got pregnant out of wedlock – was no longer welcome in decent society. DROs take these concepts one step further, by making all the information formerly known by the local community available to the world as whole, just like credit reports. (If you prefer your information to be kept more private, DROs will doubtless offer this option.)

There are really no limits to the benefits that DROs can confer upon a free society – insurance could be created for such things as:

* a man's wife giving birth to a child that is not his own;
* a daughter getting pregnant out of wedlock;
* fertility problems for a married couple;
* ...and much more.

All of the above insurance policies would require DROs to take active steps to prevent such behaviors – the mind boggles at all the preventative steps that could be taken! The important thing to remember is that all such contracts are *voluntary*, and so do not violate the moral absolute of non-violence.

In conclusion – how does the stateless society deal with violent criminals? Brilliantly! In a stateless society, there are fewer criminals, more prevention, greater sanctions – and instant forewarning of those aiming at a life of crime by their withdrawal from the DRO system. More incentives to work, fewer incentives for a life of crime, no place to hide for rogues, and general social rejection of those who decide to operate outside of the civilized world of contracts, mutual protection and general security. And remember – governments in the 20th century caused more than 200 million deaths – are we really that worried about private hold-ups and jewelry thefts in the face of those kinds of numbers?

There is no system that will replace faulty men with perfect angels, but the stateless society, by rewarding goodness and punishing evil, will at least ensure that all devils are visible – instead of cloaking them in the current deadly fog of power, politics and propaganda.

THESE CAGES ARE ONLY FOR BEASTS...

As mentioned above, DROs are private insurance companies whose sole purpose is to mediate disputes between individuals. If you and I sign a contract, we both agree beforehand to submit any disputes we cannot resolve to the arbitration of a particular DRO. Furthermore, we may choose to allow the DRO to take action if either of us fails to abide by its decision, such as property seizure or financial penalties.

So far so good. However, a problem arises if I have no DRO contract, and turn to a life of theft, murder and arson. How can that be dealt with? Above, I suggested that DROs would simply band together to deny goods, services and contracts to violent criminals.

Some readers may be concerned about the power that DROs have in a stateless society. When describing how a stateless society could deal with murderers, we are reviewing an extreme situation, not everyday economic and social relations. A doctor might say: *if a patient has an infected leg, and you have no antibiotics, amputate the leg*. This does not mean that he advocates cutting off limbs in less serious circumstances. When I say that DROs will track violent criminals and try to deny them goods and services, I do not mean that DROs would be able to do this to just anyone. First of all, customer choice would make this impossible. A store owner can ban anyone he likes – but he cannot do so arbitrarily, or he will go out of business. Similarly, if people see a DRO acting unjustly or punitively, it will quickly find itself without customers.

The most important thing to remember is that DRO contracts are perfectly *voluntary* – and that hundreds of DROs will be constantly clamoring for our business. If we are afraid that they will turn into a myriad of quasi-police states, they have to address those fears if want they us as customers.

How will they do that? Why, through contractual obligations, of course! In order to sign us up, DROs will have to offer us instant contractual release – and lucrative cash rewards – if they ever harass us or treat us arbitrarily. As a matter of course, DRO contracts will include a provision to submit any conflicts with customers to a separate DRO *of the customers' choosing*. All this is standard fare in the reduction of contractual risk.

In other words, every person who says, "DROs *will turn into dangerous fascistic organizations*," represents a fantastic business opportunity to anyone who can address that concern in a positive manner. If you dislike the idea of DROs, just ask yourself: is there *any* way that my concerns could be alleviated? Are there *any* contractual provisions that might tempt me into a relationship with a DRO? If so, the magic of the free market will provide them. Some DROs will offer to pay you a million dollars if they treat you unjustly – and *you* can choose the DRO that makes that decision! Other DROs will band together and form a review board which regularly searches their warehouses for illicit arms and armies. DROs will fund "watchdog" organizations which regularly rate DRO integrity.

If none of the above appeals to you, then the DRO system is clearly not for you – but then neither is the current State system, which is already one-sided, repressive and dictatorial. And remember – in a free society such as I describe, you can always choose to live without a DRO, of course, or pay for its services as needed (as I mention in "The Stateless Society") – as long as you do not start stealing and killing.

For those who *still* think DROs will become governments, I invite you to take a look at a real-world example of a DRO – one of the world's largest "employers." Currently, over 300,000 people rely on it for a significant portion of their income. Most of what they sell is so inexpensive that lawsuits are not cost-effective, and transactions regularly cross incompatible legal borders – in other words, they operate in a stateless society. So how does *eBay* resolve disputes? Simply through dialogue and the dissemination of information. If I do not pay for something I receive, I get a strike against me. If I do not ship something that I was paid for, I also get a strike. Everyone I deal with can also rate my products, service and support. If I am rated poorly, I have to sell my goods for less since, everything else being equal, people prefer dealing with a better-rated vendor (or buyer). If enough people rate me poorly, I will go out of business, because the risk of dealing with me becomes too great. There are no police or courts or violence involved here – thefts are simply dealt with through communication and information sharing.

Thus eBay is an example of the largest DRO around – are we really afraid that it is going to turn into a quasi-government? Do any of us truly lie awake wondering whether the eBay SWAT team is going to break down our doors and drag us away to some offshore J2EE coding gulag?

Any system can be abused – which is why governments are so abhorrent – and so checks and balances are essential to any proposed form of social organization. That's the beauty of the DRO approach. Those who dislike, mistrust or fear DROs do not have to have anything to do with them, and can rely on handshakes, reputation and trust – or start their own DRO. Those whose scope prohibits such approaches – multi-million dollar contracts or long-term leases come to mind – can turn to DROs. Those who are afraid of DROs becoming mini-States can set up watchdog agencies and monitor them (paid for by others who share such fears, perhaps).

In short, either the majority of human beings *can* cooperate for mutual advantage, or they cannot. If they can, a stateless society will work – especially since millions of minds far better than mine will be constantly searching for the best solutions. If they cannot, then no society will *ever* work, and we are doomed to slavery and savagery by nature.

Therefore, I stand by my thesis in "Caging the Beasts" above – if you mug, rape or kill, I will support any social action that thwarts your capacity to survive in society. I want to see you hounded into the wilderness, refused hotel rooms and groceries – and I want your face plastered everywhere, so that the innocent can stay safe by keeping you at bay. I abhor the thug as much as I abhor the State – and it is because such thugs exist that the State cannot be suffered to continue, since the State always disarms honest citizens and encourages, promotes and protects the thugs.

STATELESS DICTATORSHIPS: HOW A FREE SOCIETY PREVENTS THE RE-EMERGENCE OF A GOVERNMENT

By far the most common objection to the idea of a stateless society is the belief that one or more private Dispute Resolution Organizations (DROs) would overpower all the others and create a new government. This belief is erroneous at every level, but has a kind of rugged persistence that is almost admirable.

Here is the general objection:

In a society without a government, whatever agencies arise to help resolve disputes will inevitably turn into a replacement government. These agencies may initially start as competitors in a free market, but as time goes by, one will arise to dominate all the others economically, and will then wage war against its competitors, and end up imposing a new State upon the population. The instability and violence that this "DRO civil war" will inflict upon the population is far worse than any existing democratic State structure. Thus, a

stateless society is far too risky an experiment, since we will just end up with
a government again anyway!

This objection to an anarchic social structure is considered self-evident, and thus is never presented with actual proof. Naturally, since the discussion of a stateless society involves a future theoretical situation, empirical examples cannot apply.

However, like all propositions involving human motivation, the "replacement state" hypothesis can be subjected to logical examination.

Premises

The basis of the "replacement state" hypothesis is the premise that people prefer to maximize their income with the lowest possible expenditure of energy. The motivation for a DRO to use force is that, by eliminating all competition and taking military control of a geographical region, a DRO can make much more money than through free market competition, and that it is worth it to invest resources in military conflict in order to secure the permanent revenue source of a new tax base.

We can fully accept this premise, as long as it is applied consistently to *all* human beings in a stateless society. To make the "replacement state" case even stronger, we will also assume that no moral scruples could conceivably get in the way of any decision-making. By reducing the "drive to dominate" to a mere calculation of economic efficiency, we can eliminate any possible ethical brakes on the situation.

Starting Point

Let us start with a stateless society, wherein citizens can voluntarily choose to contract with a DRO for the sake of property protection and dispute resolution. Each citizen also has the right to break his contract with his DRO.

There are essentially three possible ways that a DRO could gain military control of an entire region:

1. By secretly amassing an army, and then suddenly unleashing it upon all competitors;
2. By *openly* amassing an army, and then doing the same thing;
3. By posing as a voluntary "Defense DRO," amassing arms supposedly for the legitimate defense of citizens, and then turning those arms against the citizens and instituting itself as a new government.

There is one additional possibility, which is that a private citizen can try to assemble his own army.

Let's deal with each of these in turn.

The Secret Army

In this scenario, let's say that a DRO manager called "Bob" decides that he is tired of dealing with customers on a voluntary basis. He decides he is going to spend company money buying enormous amounts of armaments and training an army. (For the moment, let us assume that Bob can make this decision entirely on his own, and does not need to submit to any sort of Board, bank or investor review.)

Let us assume that Bob's DRO has annual revenues of $500 million a year, and profits of $50 million a year.

The most immediate challenge that Bob is going to face is: *how on earth am I going to pay for an army?* Given that, in a free society, there is no way of knowing exactly how many citizens are armed – or what kinds of weapons they have – it would be necessary to err on the side of caution and assemble a fairly prodigious and overwhelming army to gain control of an entire region, otherwise Bob's investment would be entirely lost in a military defeat. Such armies are scarcely cheap. For the purposes of this argument, let's say that it is going to cost $500 million over five years for Bob to assemble his army – surely a lowball estimate. How is he going to get the money to pay for this?

Raising Rates

The most obvious way for Bob to raise the extra $500 million is to charge his customers more. The $500 million Bob needs represents more than 10 years of his DROs annual profits of $50 million a year (reinvesting the $50m for 5 years at 10% yields $805.26m). Thus, in order to pay for his army within five years, Bob is going to have to more than *double* his prices. Since we have already assumed that it is Bob's *greed* that makes him want to create a new government – and that this greed is common to all citizens within the society – we can also assume that his customers share his motivation. Thus, just as Bob *wants* to have an army so that he can maximize his income, his customers just as surely do *not* want Bob to have an army, for exactly the same reasons. The moment that Bob informs his customers that he will now be charging them more than double for exactly the same services, he will lose all his customers, and go out of business. Sadly, no army for Bob.

Full Disclosure

Perhaps, though, Bob recognizes this danger, and plans to keep his customers by telling them that he is raising their rates *in order* to fund an army. "Help me buy an army by paying me double your current rates," he tells them, "and I will share the plunder I'll get when I take over such-and-such a neighborhood!" Even if we assume that Bob's customers believe him, and are willing to fund such a mad scheme, Bob's secret is now out, and society as a whole – including *all* the other DROs – have been informed of Bob's nefarious intentions. Clearly, all the other DROs will immediately cease doing business with Bob's DRO. Since a central value of any DRO is its ability to interact with other DROs – just as a core value of a cell phone company is its ability to interact with other cell phone companies – Bob's DRO will thus be crippled. In other words, Bob will be more than doubling his rates for many years – while providing a far inferior service – for a highly uncertain and dangerous "profit."

In addition, Bob's bank would immediately cease doing business with him, rendering him unable to pay his employees, his office rental, or his bills. Bob's electricity company will cease supplying electricity, he will find his taps strangely dry, his phones will be cut off, and many other misfortunes will arise as a result of his stated desire to become a new dictator. It is hard to imagine him lasting five days, let alone retaining all of his paying customers at double the rates for the five years required to build his army!

Even if all the above problems could somehow be overcome, it is hard to imagine that Bob's customers would be happy to arm Bob in the hopes of sharing in his plunder. Unlike the government, which can tax at will, DROs must *actually* protect their customer's property in order to retain their business. Given that those who contract with DROs are those with the most interest in protecting their property, it makes little sense that they would fund Bob's DRO army, since they would have no actual control with that army once it was created, and thus no way of enforcing any "plunder contract" created beforehand. In a free society, people would not try to "protect" their property by funding a powerful army that could then take it away from them at will. *That* sort of madness requires the existence of a government!

Alternative Funding

Perhaps Bob will try to fund his army in other ways. He may try and borrow the money, but his bank will only lend him the money if he comes up with a credible and measurable business plan. If Bob's business plan openly states his desire to create an army, his bank would cease supporting him in any way, shape or form, since the bank would only stand to lose if such an army were created. If Bob took the money from the bank by submitting a fraudulent business plan, the bank would be aware of this almost immediately, and would take the remainder of the money back – and impose stiff penalties on Bob to boot! Again, no army for Bob.

What if Bob tried to pay for his army by reducing the dividends he was paying to shareholders? Naturally, the shareholders would resent this, and would either have him thrown out, or would simply sell their shares and invest their money elsewhere, thus crippling Bob's DRO. Perhaps Bob would try paying his employees less, but that would only drive his employees into the arms of other DROs – also destroying his business.

It is safe to say that it is practically impossible for Bob to get the money to pay for his army – and even if he got such money, his business would never survive such a dangerous transgression of social and economic norms.

There are other dangers, however, which are well worth examining.

Defense DROs

The most likely threat would seem to come from "Defense DROs," since those agencies would already have weapons and personnel that might be used against the general population. However, this would be very difficult for two main reasons. First, "Defense DROs" would require investment and banking relationships in order to grow and flourish. Given that investors and banks would not want to fund an army that could steal their property, they would be certain to insert myriad "fail-safe" mechanisms into their "Defense DRO" contracts. They would make sure that all arms purchases were tracked, that all monies were accounted for, and that no secret armies were being assembled.

"Defense DROs" would also be subject to the same kinds of funding problems as Bob's DRO. Let's say that Dave is the head of a "Defense DRO," and wakes up one day seized by the desire to assemble his own army and pillage society.

First of all, citizens would never contract with any "Defense DRO" that would not submit to regular audits of its weapons and accounts to ensure that no secret armies were being created. If Dave decides to bypass this contractual obligation, and start secretly funding his own army, how is he going to pay for it? The moment he raises his rates without increasing his services, his customers will know exactly what he's up to, and withdraw their support. Bye-bye army. Dave's funding would also be subject to all the other problems raised above.

It can thus be seen that there is no viable way for any DRO to pay for a secret army without destroying its business in the process. Armies are only really possible when the government can force taxpayers to subsidize them.

INDEPENDENTLY WEALTHY?

Perhaps, instead of Bob or Dave, we have a privately wealthy individual named Bill, a multibillionaire who decides to raise an army and institute himself as a new dictator. Due to his immense wealth, he is not dependent on any customers, employees, or shareholders. Let us say that he can pay for an army out of his own pocket, immediately.

Bill's challenge, of course, is that in a free society, he cannot exactly pick up a complete army at his local Wal-Mart. Armies are fundamentally uneconomical, expensive overhead at best, and thus it seems likely that geographical defense in a free society would be limited to a couple of dozen nuclear weapons, to deter any potential invader. Thus even if he could get a hold of one, buying a nuke would not help Bill very much, since he would be unable to use it to overwhelm all of the other "Defense DROs."

What about more conventional weapons? Part of the service that "Defense DROs" would offer to subscribers would be a guarantee that they would do everything in their power to prevent the rise of an independent army – either of their own making, or of anyone else's. Thus arms manufacturers would have to provide rigorous accounts of everything they were making and selling, to be sure that they weren't selling arms to some secret army, probably in the foothills of Montana. If people were really worried about the possibility of someone creating a private army, they would only do business with "Defense DROs" that guaranteed that they bought their arms from open and legitimate arms dealers – subject to independent verification, of course.

Thus when Bill came along trying to buy $500 million worth of weapons, and hire an army of tens of thousands of soldiers, one question would be: *where on earth would they come from?* Arms manufacturers would not be sitting on $500 million of inventory, due to the limited demand for such products, and the costs of making and storing them. Thus the arms manufacturers would have to really crank up their production, which could not be hidden from the general population, or the Defense DROs that such extra production would directly threaten. In order to make all the extra armaments, manufacturers would have to borrow money to expand production. Where would they get this extra money from? Their banks would surely not fund such a dangerous endeavor, and would immediately notify any Defense DROs it had contracts with, and drop the rogue arms manufacturer as a customer. Defense DROs and general customers would also never do business with such a dangerous arms manufacturer ever again, thus driving it out of business.

No manufacturer would ever expand production for a "one time" purchase, any more than you would buy a car to make a single trip. Also – why would an arms manufacturer sell deadly weapons to a private individual, knowing that this individual would be able to use those arms to steal more weapons from the manufacturer?

Secondly, even if Bill could somehow get his hands on the necessary weapons, where would these tens of thousands of new troops come from? In a stateless society, the military would not be exactly the same kind of "in demand" career that it is today. In order to assemble an army of tens of thousands of men, Bill would have to advertise, recruit, pay them, train them, etc. This would be impossible to hide. Since it would be completely obvious that Bill was assembling an army, what could people in society conceivably do to stop him?

First of all, if this were a potential risk, his bank would have a clause in its service agreement giving it the right to refuse to honor any payments clearly designed to fund a private army. Secondly, no DRO would do business with Bill – or his soldiers – the moment that it became apparent what he was up to. This would mean that none of Bill's soldiers would have any guarantees that they would get paid, grocery stores would not sell them food, electricity companies would cut them off, gas stations would not sell them gas, etc. When society as a whole wants to stop doing business with you, it becomes very hard to get by.

THE QUESTION OF PROFIT

Remember, we began this section with the premise that someone would want an army in order to make money. Let us see if this can be achieved, even if all the above obstacles can somehow be overcome.

Let us say that our first friend "Bob" *can* somehow get his army – the question is: can he make that army pay?

Remember, it cost Bob $500 million over five years to assemble his army – let us say that it costs another $1 billion over the next five years to subdue a reasonably-sized region, due to the loss of life and equipment involved in combat. What kinds of financial returns can Bob expect?

If you know that Bob's army is going to be at your house in two weeks, and there is no way to stop it, you would just pull a "scorched-earth Russian defense" and leave, right? You would take everything of value with you, and perhaps destroy everything that you could not bring. Thus, what would Bob's army end up getting control of? Not much.

However, let us imagine that Bob's army *could* somehow seize assets that would be worth something. How much would they have to steal in order to make a profit?

First, let us look at the alternatives, or the *opportunity costs* of Bob's army.

Bob has to invest $100 million each year over five years to assemble his army – what does that cost him overall?

If Bob invested the $100 million back into his DRO instead, he will likely get 10% ROI. In five years of compound returns, that translates to $832.61m.

Then, Bob has to invest *another* billion dollars over the next five years invading a series of neighborhoods. How much does that really cost him? $1,665.22m, or $1 billion invested at 10% over five years. But that's not all – the $832.61m above would *also* have gained 10% per year over the remaining 5 years, resulting in a total of $1,340.93m.

Thus Bob's five years of preparation and five years of military rampaging have cost him over *$3 billion*. Given the enormous risks involved in such an endeavor, investors would likely demand at least a 20:1 pay off – similar to the software field. Thus Bob would have to steal well over *$60 billion*, given that he would likely want to keep some money for himself.

Where would this $60 billion come from? The burned-out houses? The abandoned cars? It is hard to imagine that anything Bob got his hands on would be worth very much at all.

(The evidence of history tends to support this conclusion. Economically, imperialism is a disaster for everyone except those intimately connected to the coercive power of the State.)

Also, Bob has wrecked an economy that was enabling him to generate a 10% annual return on his investments – even if he steals billions of dollars, it would *still* be less than he would have received over the course of his life if he had just re-invested his money! Reinvestment also carries with it the considerable advantage of not exposing Bob to the risk of death through assassination or war.

What if Bob wanted to spring a surprise attack on citizens and start taxing them? Again, all the other DROs would stand to lose all their customers in such an event, and so would take all necessary steps to prevent it from occurring. They would have to provide innovative "checks and balances" solutions to potential customers in order to win them as clients, ensuring their collective vigilance against such surprise attacks. Furthermore, given that there are no borders in a stateless society, those that Bob's army encircled would just abscond in the middle of the night, fleeing his predations.

However, even if *all* of the above problems can be somehow overcome, and the creation of a rogue army in a free society could become both possible *and* profitable, the solution to this danger is simple. Any "Defense DRO" would simply buy the trust of its clients by promising to pay them a fine in excess of any potential military profits if that DRO was ever discovered to be assembling an army. As mentioned above, DROs would simply put millions of dollars in trust, payable to any customer that could find evidence proving that a rogue army was being created. Problem solved.

When we look at the series of steps required to make the creation of a private "rogue" army economically profitable, we can see that it becomes so unlikely as to be functionally impossible. If we assume that the economic incentive of maximizing profits would drive someone to consider such a course, we can easily see that the fears of inevitable private tyrannies are merely imaginary.

The "replacement state" mythology is just another ghost story invented to keep us in cages whose bars are merely fictional.

IRRATIONAL LAWS?

Another question that constantly arises about anarchistic social organization is the degree to which different communities will create or maintain unjust or irrational rules. What would stop an Islamic community from imposing Sharia law, or a particular group that wishes to raise their children communally, or have multiple spouses, or ban the wearing of red clothing?

This is of course possible, but there are several tendencies within an anarchic society that will discourage and eliminate such obtuse practices in the long run.

First of all, though, it is important to understand that there is no real solution for this in a statist society – assuming it is not a dictatorship. As long as we do not aggress against others, if a group of friends and I wish to get together and live in an enormous house, share all our property and live in some polyamorous hippie flesh-pile, there is nothing illegal about this in a statist society. As long as our children are fed, cared for and educated, we can all choose to live common-law and raise our children collectively if we want.

Similarly, if a group of Muslims wish to live according to Sharia rules, and everyone voluntarily accepts these rules and lives by them of their own free will, there is very little that a stateless society can do about that either. Since governments only have violence and pro-paganda to maintain their rule, they can only send SWAT teams in to break up communes, or tanks and helicopters to dismember religious groups – but very few of us would applaud that as a reasoned and positive response to the challenges of varying beliefs within society.

Economically, a stateless society is fundamentally characterized by an *inability for particular groups to violently offload the costs of their preferences onto others.*

If you are part of a group that wishes to invade Iraq, for instance you will have to find a way to fund that yourself – you will not be able to print money or tax others to pay for your preferences. Do any of us truly believe that the chicken-hawks in the current political administration would have decided to commit genocide against the Iraqi population if they had been sent the multi-trillion dollar bill for the evils they contemplated? Would any purely private financial institution have funded such a monstrous invasion? Of course not – war is impossible without taxation.

The most economically efficient legal system is the one which extends reasonable resources to prevent problems before they occur – and then sits inert until someone complains about an injustice.

The DRO system is wonderful at preventing problems, since it inherently contains all sorts of red flags for potential criminal behavior, as described above. What do I mean by saying that it will very likely sit in an inert state?

Let us look at gambling as an example.

Gambling – though obviously potentially addictive – is a voluntary transaction between adults. In any reasonable legal system, where there is consent, there can be no crime. A man may complain if he loses his shirt at a roulette table, but he cannot claim that he was the victim of force or fraud.

If we understand this, we can see that there is an enormous difference between a *proactive* and a *reactive* legal system. A reactive legal system waits patiently until it receives a complaint about an injustice – then, it leaps into action to provide justice.

A *proactive* legal system sends armed men out in waves, ferreting and rooting around in society in order to capture and punish adults interacting in a voluntary and peaceful manner. This kind of legal system is an ugly stepchild of the Spanish Inquisition, and arises out of a hysterical form of aggressive moral puritanism, generally religious in origin. In this kind of legal system, an absence of force or fraud is not enough to allow people to escape moral condemnation, capture and punishment. These "voluntary crimes" tend to revolve around mind-altering substances, gambling and prostitution, and are often instigated in a statist society by women who find out that they have married the wrong men (the Women's Christian Temperance Union etc.)

Activities which certain people find distasteful are ferreted out and punished not because the participants find them evil or immoral, but because others do. The man who smokes some vegetation, gambles some money, or pays for sex obviously is not the criminal complainant – neither is the person who sells him weed, casino chips or sex. Instead, it is others who wish to wreak their moral vengeance upon such transgressions.

Mencken once wrote: "Puritanism: The haunting fear that someone, somewhere, may be happy." As a philosopher, I do not counsel or believe that drugs, gambling or visiting prostitutes is a recipe for long-term happiness and wisdom – but I also understand that unwise or ill-considered actions are not solved by the initiation of violence.

The insertion of this "third party" into a legal system – the entity that brings charges in the absence of complaints by any individuals in a transaction – is very, very expensive. Can you imagine how expensive it would be for a computer company to send someone over to your house every time you wanted to install a program, to make sure you got it right? Compare this to the cost of your average *reactive* tech support call center – it would be hundreds – if not thousands – of times more expensive.

There are many people who find it highly objectionable that other people enjoy taking mind-altering substances – how many of them would be willing to fund the true cost of their outrage themselves?

In the United States, the Drug Enforcement Agency budget for 2007 was over $2.3 *billion*. If we imagine that there are perhaps 25 million taxpaying adults in America who are virulently anti-drug, would they remain as virulently opposed to drugs if each of them received a bill for $100 a year? What about the approximately $100 per year that it costs to incarcerate the resulting prisoners, and the $100 in other law enforcement costs? Overall, the war on drugs costs over $20 billion a year - $800 for each of the 25 million taxpaying adults who find drugs so objectionable.

How many of these people would find themselves somehow magically able to manage a "live and let live" attitude towards drug consumption if they were sent an $800 bill every single year? Can we imagine that 50% of them would drop out? If so, then the remaining 12.5 million people would be sent a bill for $1,600 – how many of them would drop out that this rate? Half? Very well – then the remaining would be sent a bill for $3,200 – and so on, until the last man to be sent the bill for $20 billion somehow found it in his heart to avoid the bill by embracing tolerance and compassion.

The "drug war" (which is a war of course on people, not drugs) would inevitably collapse if those who found drugs so objectionable actually had to pay for their moral outrage themselves.

Similarly, enforcing Sharia law requires just such a proactive legal system, which is horrendously expensive relative to a reactive legal system. How long would such religious intransigence last if the fanatics had to pay for their mania themselves, and faced competition from perfectly functional legal systems that charged one tenth the cost?

Proactive legal systems are prohibitively expensive, unless the costs can be violently extracted from others. In this way, we know for certain that proactive legal systems would have a very short lifespan in a stateless society, and that the natural justice of reactive legal systems would very quickly become – and remain – the norm.

What is commonly called "culture," in other words, is most often little more than a set of violently subsidized and irrational prejudices.

TANK CONTROL

Two other questions that arise about anarchism is the "tank in the garden" problem and the question of gun control. I have kept these examples in the "Reasoning" section because the answers to these questions pertain so many other questions as well.

THE TANK IN THE GARDEN

This objection runs something along these lines:

"Let us suppose that you have a neighbor who becomes obsessed with military hardware, and begins building a tank in his backyard. It looks like a very realistic tank, and he even gets a hold of shells. He then drives the tank back and forth in his backyard, and points the turret directly at your house. Clearly, this is not a good situation for you, but your neighbor is only exercising his own property rights, and so what right do you have to interfere with his tank-building? Certainly, if he accidentally blows the top off your house, you can act in response, but surely you should not have to wait for such a disaster in order to intervene – forcefully, if necessary."

If we believe that anarchism is a society without rules or laws, then this would seem to be a perplexing problem. In a statist society, you simply have laws against private tank ownership, and the problem is solved!

However, as we have discussed above, anarchism is not a society without rules or laws, but is rather populated by agencies entirely devoted to preventing foreseeable problems. Some problems are complicated and hard to detect – but the "tank in the garden" is not one of those problems. Furthermore, if we are so concerned about military hardware being used against us, it scarcely seems a wise "solution" to arm a government to the teeth, and disarm ourselves proportionately.

If people are afraid of the "tank in the garden," all they have to do is ensure that their DRO contract contains protections against well-armed neighbors. How can this be achieved? Well, when my wife and I bought our house, we signed a contract stipulating that we were not to repaint the outside of our house for a period of five years. I am sure that we would not have hesitated to sign the contract if it also included a ban on building tanks, nuclear weapons and aircraft carriers.

If someone does break their DRO contract by building such weapons, the DRO can invoke all of the exclusion and ostracism penalties discussed above.

Gun Control

Some people prefer to live in neighborhoods where there are no guns; some people prefer to live in neighborhoods where everyone has a gun – and some people do not particularly care one way or the other. Anarchism perfectly satisfies everyone's preferences in this area. If you are a developer building a new neighborhood, you can require everyone buying a house to sign a contract promising to refrain from owning a gun. The enforcement possibilities for this are endless, but need not be intrusive – if I were a DRO and wanted to prevent gun ownership, I would simply revoke my contract with anyone who used or showed a gun in the neighborhood – including acts of self-defense.

On the other hand, I could build a neighborhood which required that everyone be willing to have and know how to use a gun – as is already the case in Switzerland. If I believe that gun ownership in a net positive, I would buy a house in this neighborhood.

Ah, but what if you have a gun in the glove box of your car, and you are driving from neighborhood to neighborhood? Well, then, you are just taking a risk that if you are discovered, your DRO may revoke your contract, just as if you carry a concealed weapon against the law in a statist society. Or they may not care about drivers.

In general, it seems very likely that few if any gun restrictions would be in place in a stateless society. The level of crime would be at *least* 90% lower than it is today; children would grow up happier, better educated and more secure – and of course you do not need to actually own a gun in order to gain the protective benefits of gun ownership. A thief who wants to break into your house does not know in advance whether you have a gun or not – if everyone is legally disarmed, then he can be quite sure that you do not. However, in a stateless society, there are no "laws" against gun ownership, except those that people enter into voluntarily. If a large number of thieves somehow figure out how to operate in an anarchic society, they will inevitably be drawn to those neighborhoods which have anti-gun contracts, so they will face less risk during their robberies. If these crimes become prevalent, then randomized gun ownership would be the most optimal solution – if these crimes remain extraordinarily rare, as is most likely the case, insofar as only the mentally ill would attempt them, then gun ownership would become an unnecessary overhead, and would very likely decline to almost nothing. There would still be people who would own guns, but they would be a small minority of eccentric collectors, like those who collect medieval swords – legacies of a brutal past that has long since faded into history.

PART 3

Examples

• • •

ROADS

THE QUESTION OF ROADS ALWAYS seems to arise as a central objection to a stateless society – which makes perfect sense in a way, because it is a form of public ownership that we have all experienced firsthand, and because it can be hard to picture what they may look like in the absence of a government.

The alternative to state-funded roads is generally conceived to be toll-based roads. This is considered a disastrous solution, because who wants to stop every block to put a quarter in a meter?

Remembering our methodology from above, it is essential that we put ourselves into the mind of a road developer, sitting on the other side of that table, attempting to sell *us* access to his roads.

Imagine that you have sunk your life savings into building a complicated network of roads. If you don't attract drivers who are willing to pay to use them, you are finished – your children are going to cry themselves to sleep with hunger.

When you stand up to make a presentation to a group of potential customers – drivers – are you seriously going to tell them that in order to drive a half a mile to pick up a loaf of bread, they are going to have to stop a few times to put quarters into a toll meter?

Of course not.

So – how are you going to convince drivers to use your roads?

For those who have not spent any time – or blood – in the entrepreneurial world, this is exactly how almost all companies are funded. You take your business venture to a group of investors, who play a very serious game of "devil's advocate," trying to find holes in your business plan.

If your entire fortune hung in the balance, how would you answer these objections? If you cannot provide good answers, you will never get to sell your roads.

I am certainly no expert in construction – I was an entrepreneur in the software world – but I can tell you some possible answers that I would explore in order to prepare for such a meeting. I can also tell you that none of them would involve having drivers stop every few minutes to push change into a slot.

If I desperately wanted to build roads in a stateless society, I would first approach construction companies who wanted to build houses or malls in some area not currently served by a road. If you want to build a mall a few miles out of town, you're not likely to attract many investors unless your business plan includes road access to the mall, since there are very few people who enjoy the prospect of a bracing hike to and from a "Target" store.

If you are developing a housing complex, you will face exactly the same requirement – it is true that you can sell houses without road access, but you will not be able to sell them for more than it costs to build them.

So there are really two kinds of roads, in two kinds of environments – highways and intercity roads, and already-existing and new roads.

New Roads

It is easy for us to understand that highways to new places will be built in the free market, for the simple reason that if you cannot build a highway to that new place, that new place will never come into existence. Secondly, there is not much point building a highway to a new housing development, without building roads from the highway to and within the housing development.

Thus, anything that is built that is new will only be built if roads to access it are constructed at the same time.

If I want to buy a new house somewhere outside of town, and a new highway and new roads are built to accommodate my desire, I will certainly be very interested in the long-term quality of the roads that have been built, since so much of my property's value hinges upon easy and comfortable access to it.

Thus, the long-term quality of these roads will be a significant factor – probably a deciding one – in my decision to buy a house. Road quality is as important as the house's construction quality when it comes to evaluating the value of a property. How much would you pay for a million-dollar mansion in the middle of the Amazon forest, with no road access? Assuming you are not Howard Hughes, probably nothing at all.

What about the danger that someone sells me a house, and then jacks up the price of the road maintenance?

Knowing that this is a risk, when I was negotiating my mortgage, I would ensure that a built-in and fixed price for road maintenance was included in my mortgage terms. I would also want the right to demand an open bid on road maintenance services when the contract came up for renewal.

We can all understand that the construction and maintenance of new buildings – commercial or residential – can only occur with high quality road access. (We can see this kind of phenomenon, to a smaller degree, in the fact that almost no malls are built without parking spaces, or houses without driveways and garages.)

So really, the question of road construction and maintenance – as far as it is raised as an objection to a stateless society – only hinges on *existing* roads, not new ones.

The Statist Pony

Imagine some communist country which provided out of the public purse a pony for each girl on her sixteenth birthday. Now, imagine that some crazy capitalist thinker came along and said that this country should switch from communism to the free market.

Naturally, just about everyone would then demand: "But how will each girl get a free pony on her sixteenth birthday?"

Of course, the answer is that she will not – but it may very well be asked whether the pony is really such an absolute necessity for every girl.

Government roads are just such a kind of "statist pony" – they are extravagantly wasteful, badly planned and allocated, and facilitate all sorts of dangerous and inefficient behaviors, just like every other government program on the planet. There is thus no possibility that a free market system of roads will look exactly the same as a statist system – because drivers will have to pay for road use directly, rather than offloading the total costs to taxpayers as a whole.

Thus when picturing a free system of roads, the question becomes: what will we as drivers be happy to pay for?

Certainly we will pay for safety, which we currently do not receive. We get jolting and wasteful traffic lights instead of gentle and fluid roundabouts. We get endless predatory ticketing instead of road systems that promote safety. We get endless construction that does not take place in the dark of night, but rather in the agonizing slow motion of rush hour. We get a sagging expansion of our cities, because developers do not have to pay for the costs of the roads that lead to their houses, office buildings, factories and shopping malls. We get eighteen-wheeler trucks blaring and rocketing beside small passenger cars. We do not see businesses adapting to the monetary and social costs of rush hour, because they do not face increased demand in wages because traveling in rush-hour costs more. Thus everyone has to start at nine a.m. or thereabouts.

Like every other government program, roads and traffic control are run for the profit of special interests – construction companies, unions, bureaucrats and cops, primarily – and not for the sake of the end users, the drivers. The tens of thousands of deaths – and hundreds of thousands of injuries – that occur annually in the United States alone, would be a completely unacceptable body count in any private industry. Experiments such as roundabouts, removing traffic signs and lanes, charging a premium for high-volume traffic and so on – all of which have been proven to increase efficiency and safety – simply do not spread across the system, any more than salmon steaks showed up in your average Stalinist store.

Existing City Roads

No matter what happens to the highway system in general, we all appreciate that city roads have to be maintained. How can this happen without a toll at every corner?

If we look at the average downtown core, it is largely composed of shops and businesses. Is it beyond the pale of human thought to imagine that the stores and businesses on a particular city block would be able to get together and all chip in for a relatively modest fund to maintain the roads and sidewalks around them – particularly when they no longer have to pay property and profit taxes to the State?

If we do believe that this is impossible, then we face exactly the same problem that we faced before about democracy. The central idea of democracy is that citizens are able to put aside their own petty personal self-interest and vote according to their conscience, with an eye to the collective good of society. If we accept that human beings are capable of voting in this way, then surely we can accept that they can put a few bucks a month into a common pot to pay for the roads that bring customers and employees to them. If we do not think that human beings can organize themselves to take care of a few hundred meters of roads that they directly benefit from, then they will never be able to vote for political candidates with any thought for the common good, and democracy must be abolished.

Either way, we end up with a stateless society.

There are, of course, many other ways to charge for roads in a free society. GPS tracking devices can effortlessly monitor the movements of cars, and a single bill can be sent, and the proceeds apportioned out to the road companies involved.

Furthermore, non-dangerous advertising could very easily subsidize the cost of roads – one possibility that springs to mind is radio commercials that would be inserted into programs based on the location of drivers, so that they did not provide visual distractions.

A Predatory Road Monopoly?

All right, you may say, but what about the reality that highways – and city roads – are extremely non-competitive situations, since no one is going to build a highway next to another highway and compete with it?

That is somewhat true, although it is important to be precise in terms of what is meant by the word "competition."

Brad Pitt has a monopoly on Brad Pitt – or at least, he did before he got married. However, Brad Pitt still faces competition – not just with other actors, but rather with everything else that human beings could be doing instead of going to see a Brad Pitt movie. He competes with bowling, sex, napping, reading books on anarchy – everything you could imagine! Thus, although he has a monopoly on Brad Pitt, he does not have a monopoly on *you*. (That is the difference between the government and the free market – the government *does* have a monopoly on you, because it initiates the use of force against you.)

In the same way, any particular highway may have a monopoly on getting from A to B in the straightest line – but that does not mean that it has a coercive and exclusive hold over everyone's entire decision-making processes.

Let us take an example of an "evil capitalist highway robber baron" named Jacques, who decides to start jacking up the rates for any driver using his highway.

First of all, Jacques will not be making this decision in a vacuum. After roads become privatized, everyone who buys a house who relies on a particular highway will be fully aware of their vulnerability to increased road tolls in the future. As an enterprising construction capitalist, I would sweeten the pot for people in this regard by negotiating a twenty year guarantee with Jacques that he would not raise their prices any more than one or two percentage points a year. (This highlights again a very essential aspect of understanding how a stateless society works, which is that obvious worries will always be addressed and alleviated ahead of time. If people are afraid that someone is going to jack up their road prices, they will simply negotiate fixed fees ahead of time – which is the essence of mortgages and car payments of course.)

However, let us imagine that no binding contracts limit Jacques's ability to raise his prices, and one day he announces that his rates are going to triple.

What happens then?

Well, people are not about to move because the price of their road travel is going up, so that is not likely to be an issue – what they *will* do, however, is go to their bosses and say that they need a raise.

Bosses – having been one myself – are notoriously cheap individuals, who do not want to pay a penny more than they have to for what they want. If I were a boss in this situation, I would explore other alternatives to giving raises.

For instance, I might offer them a day or two a week to work at home. Alternatively, since no doubt Jacques's prices are higher during rush-hour, I would also offer more flexible hours to those who wanted them, so that they would not have to pay a premium to come to work at a specific time.

If I were another kind of entrepreneur, I would set up a website dedicated to helping people find carpooling, so that people would end up paying less.

Also, the increased prices per vehicle might very well make it economically viable to start running buses along the highway.

In this way, Jacques might gain a temporary increase in his revenues, but consumers would simply adapt to his increased prices, in such a way that this increase could not be both significant and permanent.

In other words, by drastically raising his prices, all that Jacques is really doing is teaching people to find alternatives to using his highway. He is training them to avoid his service – and one of the terrible aspects of this practice is that once people get used to working at home or car pooling, not all of them will revert to their old habits if he drops his prices.

Jacques also creates another significant risk, which can easily escape the inexperienced eye.

By increasing the price of his highway, Jacques has reduced the collective wealth of entire neighborhoods to a far greater degree than he has increased his own wealth specifically. Of course, no one expects Jacques to be motivated by some abstract considerations of social wealth, but nonetheless he is creating a very dangerous situation.

Almost all neighborhoods have some sort of Business Association, where members meet to discuss a variety of collective concerns. This Association will certainly meet – and pointedly *not* invite Jacques – a day or two after he jacks up his prices, in order to figure out what they should do. They will likely decide to ostracize Jacques, which will certainly have a negative effect on his ability to move with ease and profit in the business world, since so many deals are consummated through existing relationships.

It is very possible that this form of business ostracism will cost Jacques more than he can possibly make by raising his rates, especially after the inevitable consumer adaptation.

However, perhaps Jacques doesn't care about these particular business relationships – it does not matter, his ability to do business is *still* irretrievably harmed.

Whomever Jacques wants to do business with next will be fully aware that he has a habit of outrageously jacking up his prices without warning. Therefore, if someone has a choice about doing business with Jacques, he will very likely refrain.

Anyone who does end up wanting to – or having to – do business with Jacques will have to do far more due diligence and legal wrangling than before his fears were elevated by Jacques's deleterious and unpredictable business practices.

Thus it is enormously unlikely that jacking up his prices will end up having a permanent and positive effect on Jacques's profits.

However, to take the argument to its extreme case, let us say that Jacques *does* somehow end up creating a permanent and positive enormous profit.

His actions have created a large number of business people who have a direct interest in reducing those prices again – all those people whose property values and business expenses have been negatively impacted by Jacques's price increase.

The Business Association members would be highly motivated to plot and execute a takeover of Jacques's highway business, in order to restore their own property and business values. Whatever debts they may incur in this process will be more than recompensed by the increase in these values. Since the personal profits that Jacques is accruing remain far less than the collective costs he is inflicting on others, he remains highly vulnerable and exposed to a takeover bid, either hostile or friendly.

Of course, the Business Association members are unlikely to be experts at running a highway, so they would more likely act as investors for competing highway companies, to fund an expansion takeover, on the condition that this new company would guarantee a return to the original rates, along with a longer-term guarantee of reasonable rate increases.

Thus in general the instability, customer alienation, ostracism and endless competitive risks introduced by sudden and large price increases do not pay off at all, and in fact threaten the viability of the business as a whole. In the example above, we have simplified the scenario by pretending that Jacques can make all of these decisions on his own, which would never be the case in any free market. Any industry that has a potential for a monopoly would require a large amount of capital investment and management, which comes with stockholders, investors, and a board of directors. Jacques would not have the right or the ability to make significant decisions about price without the support of the majority of the interested stakeholders – all of whom would view, and quite rightly too, the jacking up of prices as far too threatening to the long-term value of their investment.

My Way or the Highway?

We could imagine a scenario where Jacques is able to build a $500 million dollar highway out of his own pocket, because he has inherited billions or something like that – but it seems very unlikely that his venture would succeed in the long run, because people would be hesitant to get into business with someone who does not have a multitude of other interested parties to temper his judgment, and who retains a tyrannical level of control over his own organization. For instance, people do not want to get heavily involved in a company without a succession plan, and having a single "dictator" in a company does not bode well for its long-term success. If Jacques is not actively grooming a number of successors, and if he then gets hit by a bus, no one will be able to step into his shoes, and his company will fail. This level of risk would be too high for most other companies, since it would take a number of years to build his highway, and Jacques's company could collapse at any time, leaving bills unpaid and orders unfulfilled. If Jacques insisted upon these conditions, all that he would be revealing would be his own lack of business judgment, which would also cause more experienced businesspeople to shy away from getting involved with him. Thus it seems exceedingly unlikely that Jacques would be able to build such a capital-intensive structure while retaining dictatorial control over the company.

I do apologize for the detailed and somewhat technical nature of the above explanation, but I do think that it is essential to understand that there are always two sides to every negotiation. In a free society, there are a near-infinite set of options available to peacefully address what could be considered sub-optimal business practices on the part of others.

Automobile Insurance

Finally, let us look at how the provision of automobile insurance would affect the safety of roads.

In most Western countries, automobile insurance is compulsory – I believe that this would continue to be the case in practice, if not in principle, in a free society.

I would much prefer to use someone's roads if I could know for certain that all the other drivers carried insurance. Thus it seems very likely that insurance would be required for anyone traveling on a road. (How could this be enforced? A number of options spring to mind, most notably that currency companies would not process gas purchases from uninsured drivers.)

Naturally, the fewer car accidents there are, the more car insurance companies can make in profit. This direct correlation is one of the core foundations to the achievement of security in a stateless society. If, say, Jacques's roads are unsafe, then the car insurance companies will charge a premium for anyone who wants to drive on them – thus cutting into Jacques's profits considerably. This will drive Jacques to invest in road improvements.

At the moment, insurance companies have no direct control over government road policies, and so these companies can only compete on price, not on the proactive promotion of road safety. However, when competition for roads heats up through privatization – and remember, the competition is not just between different road systems, but also between using roads and not using them – insurance companies will be forced to compete on creating the safest possible roads, in order to keep their prices as low as possible.

When the costs of roads are directly borne by the drivers, the benefits are both staggering and almost limitless. Without the ability to externalize the cost of roads to other taxpayers, drivers can make more informed and rational decisions about the costs and benefits of driving. Where to live, how far to commute, whether to drive in rush hour, whether to use public transit, whether to carpool, whether to work from home – all of these decisions are fundamentally driven by cost, but in a statist society, these decisions almost always turn out to be disastrous, because the simple and rational efficiency of the price mechanism is not allowed to function, to the detriment of resource consumption, the health of the environment, and the quality of life for literally hundreds of millions of people.

AN EXAMPLE OF PRIVATE ROADS

If I were to say that roads should not only be provided by the free market, but also that they should be enclosed under a roof, cooled in the summer and heated in the winter, that all stairs should in fact be escalators, that all corners should be landscaped with plants and fountains, and patrolled by security guards – surely you would say that this would be an outlandish standard, which could never be achieved in the free market.

Well – that is exactly what a mall is.

Never underestimate what the free market can provide.

HEALTH CARE

The provision or subsidization of health care is considered a foundational justification for State power, for a number of seemingly compelling reasons.

First of all, health care expenses can be both unexpected and enormous. Secondly, people undergoing an acute health crisis are scarcely in a position to negotiate, haggle and wait. If you have been hit by a bus, and are bleeding out, you will not barter with whoever arrives to treat your injuries. Thirdly, health care providers are generally considered to be in a difficult position, insofar as they almost never refuse to treat someone who arrives in the emergency room, whether that person can pay or not. Fourthly, people have certain reservations or fears about the trustworthiness of medical advice, and so wish to ensure the quality and consistency of the instructions they receive. Finally, since doctors, pharmaceutical companies and other healthcare providers currently profit from illness, rather than health, the incentives are considered reversed, in that pharmaceutical companies, for instance, are motivated to deliver medication, rather than discover alternatives to medication or prevent the problem in the first place.

The "solution" to the above problems has almost always been the creation and expansion of State power over the medical field. In all Western democracies except the United States, this has resulted in the socialization of medicine, or the creation of a fundamentally communist monopoly that is funded by the taxes generated through the efficiency and productivity of the free market. Those who are healthy are forced at gunpoint to pay for those who are sick. Furthermore, the State regulates the licensing of health care providers, creating significant legal barriers to entry to doctors, nurses and other practitioners.

The imperative of providing health care – the axiom that it is a "right" – is considered a justification for the violence of the State in a way that trumps just about every other consideration. Even those who would be willing to accept the substitution of private charities for public welfare find themselves hard-pressed to defend the idea that health care should be a for-profit industry, because of the fear that, as the song goes, "the rich stay healthy, the sick stay poor..."

Every empathetic person feels the utmost compassion for an innocent child born with some form of correctable birth defect, to poor parents perhaps, who might require tens of thousands of dollars of expert help to correct the problem. The sheer random misfortune of such a disaster truly stirs us with sympathy, because we all understand that this wounded child could easily have been us, or our own child.

Similarly, those who are born with some genetic or congenital disorder are also "unjustly" inflicted with additional medical costs, through no fault of their own. A child whose teeth just happen to grow crooked requires thousands of dollars more in dental work than a child whose teeth just happen to grow straight.

When a person is struck down by an unexpected, unanticipated or inevitable medical condition – as will happen to all of us, in the case of death itself – it feels excruciating to imagine that they would have to debate costs and benefits. Particularly in the case of parents, having to choose between the best medical care for a sick child, and the medical care that they can afford, seems brutal and inhumane. Michael Moore's documentary "Sicko," for instance, opened with the story of a man who, it is claimed, had to choose between replacing one finger or another, but could not afford both.

The vulnerability and fear that accompanies significant medical ailments should, we feel, not also be combined with cold calculations about costs and benefits. Should a man with cancer be forced to choose between chemotherapy and eating? Surely a just and compassionate society should do everything within its power to avoid inflicting such stark and ghastly choices upon its citizens.

Furthermore, since medical advice can be truly a matter of life or death, a compassionate society should take every conceivable step to ensure that medical practitioners go through a rigorous process of training and evaluation. Again, the vulnerability and fear involved in medical decisions should never be exacerbated by fears that the self-interest of the medical practitioner is not directly aligned with the self-interest of the patient.

ANARCHISM AND MEDICAL CARE

There is no question that human beings are not possessed by innate sainthood. Doctors can be abrupt, greedy, false and treacherous. Patients, as well, can be difficult, obstructive, non-compliant, litigious and hypochondriacal. They can fake injuries in order to gain unjust benefits, and can also become addicted to certain medications such as painkillers, and become dangerously manipulative.

Anarchism recognizes the empirical reality of human corruption in a way that statism simply does not. Anarchists recognize that power corrupts, while statists forever believe that power is the *cure* for corruption. Anarchists understand that the only valid and proven way to oppose human corruption is through voluntarism and competition – statists believe that the only way to oppose human corruption is to create a monopoly of violent power.

Fundamentally, anarchists believe that virtue results from a marketplace of voluntary interactions – statists believe that virtue is a dictatorial compulsion, created and maintained at the point of a gun.

Ideally, no matter what your political convictions, we can all recognize that medical care should be:

1. Focused on prevention, rather than cure;
2. As cheap as possible;
3. As competent as possible;
4. As accessible as possible;
5. Aligned with the interests of the patient.

Existing Systems

A basic law of economics is that whatever you subsidize, increases; and whatever you tax, decreases.

Statist health care "systems" follow the basic model that the doctor does not get paid when you are healthy, but only gets paid when you are sick.

In other words, the doctor has no direct economic incentive to prevent illness, but every incentive to treat it.

In statist health care systems, the doctor is paid per patient visit, not for a successful cure. Thus doctors do not make their money from *curing* patients, but rather from *seeing* patients – thus they have every economic incentive to keep consultations as short as possible, and to outsource any complicated "cures."

Furthermore, in socialized medical systems in particular, it is actually *illegal* to collect and publish information about the quality and success rates of doctors. If I find out that I have prostate cancer, I cannot possibly find out which doctor has the greatest or best success rate in curing it. (More importantly, if I have a family history of prostate cancer, I cannot find out which doctor has been most successful in *preventing* it from occurring.)

When you sit back and really think about it, this is staggering – absolutely staggering!

It is illegal to sell a food item without publishing the nutritional information. It is illegal to run a public company without publishing your financial information. It is illegal to sell a car without publishing its fuel efficiency. Hell, it is illegal to sell an item of clothing without publishing where it was made.

Every stupid and irrelevant piece of information is required by *law* – but the success rates of doctors are not only not required, but you will actually go to *jail* for collecting and publishing this information!

Why is that?

This information is violently banned in most countries for two simple reasons – firstly, in any socialized system, this information would cause a stampede of sick people towards the most effective doctors. Since access to a doctor cannot be determined by price, the waiting times for good doctors would increase exponentially, while the incomes of bad doctors would decrease. Voters would go largely insane if they could not get access to the most competent doctors, and would demand immediate changes in the system. Unfortunately, the only way to limit general access to specific doctors in a socialist medical system is to allow those doctors to raise their prices – thus eliminating the communist aspect of the system.

The second reason that this information is unavailable in most medical systems is that it is already available to particular individuals, who specifically do *not* want it to be shared among the general population.

"Two-Tiered" Health Care

Whenever the "specter" of privatized medical care is raised, every pundit on the planet starts wailing about the evils of a "two-tiered" medical system. Basically, this is the fear that if elements of privatization are introduced to a public health care system, all the good doctors will flee to the private sector, leaving a dilapidated public area.

The fascinating aspect of this scare story is that these same pundits genuinely do not seem to imagine that a "tiered" medical system does not already exist within a socialized environment.

There are in fact *four* tiers in a socialized medical system; the first is inhabited by rich and prominent people, such as politicians, media personalities, pundits and so on – who do not wait in line to get MRIs or consultations with the top specialists in the field. These people inhabit a sort of "Potemkin village" of "show medicine," and are never allowed to fall through the cracks, for fear that they may write about or describe the true realities of the system. Those in the know will direct these people to the most competent medical specialists, and ensure that they are ushered into private consultations without the indignity of having sit in a waiting room. These patients then inevitably move to the front of the line for treatment, and remain immensely satisfied with the public health care system, because they do not actually have to deal with it, but rather remain quite happy to have everyone else pay for their elite private medical care.

The second tier is composed of those who are inside – or at least near – the medical profession itself. A gentleman I know who is a psychologist received the bad news that his father had colon cancer. Because he was relatively close to the medical profession, he could call on friends and immediately find out who was the best specialist in town for this disease. Then, he introduced himself to this doctor, saying that he was a friend of so-and-so, and thus inevitably vaulted to the front of the line – and this special treatment followed his father all the way through his diagnosis and chemotherapy. He always got the best doctors, and he rarely had to wait. This is not because doctors are evil, or innately corrupt, or anything like that, but rather because it is very uncomfortable to refuse a favor to a friend – and it is in fact easier to gather and keep friends when you can do favors for them, because then they will inevitably do favors for you as well.

The third tier is composed of rich people without political or medical contacts who can fly overseas for medical treatment, to the US or other more market-driven health care environments.

The fourth tier is composed of those who are not prominent, or do not wield power, are not rich, and who also do not have contacts within or near the medical profession. These hapless souls shuffle through the public health care maze, consistently displaced by those with more power, unable to gain even a scrap of information about the quality of the care that they are receiving, waiting with numb hope for the system to grace them with an appointment, with x-rays, with treatment, with advice – lost, helpless, dependent, frightened, ignorant – with no more actual "rights" than a forgotten cow lodged in a stall awaiting antibiotics.

Since a doctor is paid to see as many of these people as possible, he will impatiently rush them through his office, spending a documented average of about eighteen seconds listening to their symptoms – and by far his most common treatment option will be to write a prescription, or refer the patient to a specialist.

There are three main reasons that he writes a prescription; the first is that it gets the patient out of his office as quickly as possible, as well as transferring the bulk of any potential liability to the pharmaceutical company. The second reason, which is directly related to first, is that pharmaceutical companies shower him with gifts and trips and seminars in order to promote their medications. The third reason is that a patient can be seen very rapidly if he or she is only coming in to get a refill of the prescription – "Are you still experiencing the same symptoms? Very well, here you go!" – thus ensuring continued high-volume billing.

Of course, referring a patient to a specialist is also a very rapid way of getting him out of your office, thus maintaining your billing rate.

The Anarchist "Solution"?

Imagine if I suggested the following as the solution to the problem of how to deliver healthcare in a stateless society:

The way that I see it working is this: one DRO should amass enough weaponry to violently drive all other medical DROs out of business. This DRO should then take about twenty percent of people's income – and kidnap or shoot them if they do not give up their money – and then provide health care as it sees fit. This same DRO should also have complete control over how many doctors there are, and how a doctor should be trained, and how a doctor should be paid. Again, if anyone attempts to become a doctor without following the detailed and lengthy rules of this DRO, they can be kidnapped and/or shot. This DRO should pay doctors per patient visit, to ensure that doctors would see as many patients as possible in any given day – and it should make sure that doctors are neither paid for successful treatments, nor penalized for any unsuccessful treatments. Doctors should not make any money whatsoever by preventing illness, but rather should get paid for treating as many illnesses as possible, as quickly as possible.

Furthermore, this DRO monopoly should be able to shoot or kidnap anyone who dares to collect and publicize any information about the success rates of its doctors.

In order to ensure that citizen feedback is available to this DRO, every couple of years, citizens should be able to appoint a representative of their choice to the Board of Directors. Whoever they choose should be paid by the existing doctors that the DRO controls, or by the pharmaceutical companies...

We could continue with this example, but I think that you can see the ridiculousness of this "solution." If I put this forward as my answer, I would receive an unbelievable tsunami of incredulous and contemptuous e-mails, wondering just what particular drugs I had been on when I described this as the best possible solution to the problem of providing health care.

Inevitably – and again, ludicrously – these same people will also deluge me with incredulous and contemptuous e-mails when I suggest privatizing the provision of health care.

How It Doesn't Work: An Analogy

In socialized medicine – as in any socialized or communistic system – the *consumers* are not the *customers*. I talked about this in terms of academia in my previous book, "Everyday Anarchy," but this reality has far more dire consequences in the realm of health care.

If automobile manufacturers were paid to produce automobiles by politicians, rather than by consumers, it is easy to imagine what the results would be. Since consumer input would be almost nonexistent, the preferences and needs of the consumer would have almost no effect on what was produced.

If this statist monopoly also supported and protected a monopolistic public sector union, can we imagine what the efficiency and productivity of these workers would be?

What if these manufacturers were paid by the number of cars that were delivered, not the quality of each car? Can we imagine what would happen to the wheels when we attempted to drive the cars off the lot?

What if these car manufacturers were also heavily subsidized by the oil and gasoline industries –and those subsidies were directly proportional to the inefficient fuel consumption of their cars? Can we imagine that they would build energy-efficient cars, or would they want to increase their income by building inefficient cars?

Does anyone ever suggest that we should nationalize car production? Yet it is impossible to have a health care system without cars – or at least ambulances – since there is no easy way to deliver doctors, medicines or patients without cars.

(We could easily make the same arguments about the software and computer industry, with even more deleterious results!)

It is hard to imagine why we would create such a horrendous system for health care, while rejecting it as ridiculous and inefficient in terms of car production.

Surely our health is far more important than our cars.

Any time a coercive agency intervenes on behalf of the consumer, that coercive agency then immediately and permanently *becomes* the consumer, and the needs and desires of the actual consumer are almost entirely eliminated from the equation.

How It Will Work

Ever since Blaise Pascal discovered the laws of probability, a singular human institution has arisen to help people deal with unpredictable risk – *insurance*.

Insurance is simply a way of playing the law of averages in order to create predictability. If one out of a hundred people is going to be randomly hit with a ten thousand dollar bill, it makes sense for everyone to have the option of paying a fixed amount of money in order to be insured against such a bill.

(Please note that in this section, I am talking about the free market insurance companies of the future, not the mercantilist semi-statist monsters of the present.)

The wonderful thing about insurance is that the interests of consumers are almost exactly aligned with the interests of providers, since both are directly motivated by the desire to decrease risk.

If I take out insurance against the dangers of smoking, the insurance company only has to pay out if I get sick from smoking – thus the insurance company will inevitably reduce my rates if I quit. In the same way, if I have taken out insurance against the danger and expense of diabetes, my insurance company will charge me less if I lose weight.

(To be slightly more precise, the insurance company does not exactly *want* me to quit smoking, but rather wants to make money out of insuring me. An insurance company can as easily make money insuring smokers as it can non-smokers – however, insurance companies know that customers are more likely to stay if their rates can be reduced, which means creating incentives to quit smoking.)

Every sane individual prefers to prevent an illness rather than cure it – and this is exactly the same motivation that drives insurance companies as well, since they make the most profit from healthy people, rather than sick people.

Thus, in a free society, insurance companies provide two essential services – one that you have to pay for, and one that you get for free.

The service that you get for free is an objective and detailed risk analysis of various lifestyle options. If you want to know how dangerous hang gliding is, all you have to do is apply for insurance, tell them that you are a hang glider, and see what happens to your rates. You do not have to sign up in order to gain detailed information about the risks your habits and hobbies incur – all you have to do is apply. Insurance companies are invaluable sources of information about relative risk, since their entire livelihood is based upon a rational and sustainable evaluation of risk.

The service that you have to pay for is the alleviation of risk by spreading it around.

(This is an enormous topic, but I would briefly like to mention that any discussion of free-market health-care provision – and insurance companies in particular – will doubtless draw comparisons to the existing system within the United States. This "system" has very little to do with the free market, in that more than fifty cents of every health care dollar is spent by the government, which violently protects a monopolistic doctor's union called the American Medical Association, and also hyper-regulates the medical field with literally hundreds of thousands of laws, rules, directives and requirements. The incentive of private profit, combined with the corrupt largesse of a public purse, is technically called "fascism," rather than freedom.)

In terms of health care, then, we can be sure that your insurance company wants to keep you as healthy as possible. The farmer who sells cows is interested in their long-term health, in a way that the butcher who disassembles them is not.

Due to this motivation, private insurance companies will be reasonably proactive in attempting to prevent health problems from developing, rather than merely curing them after they have occurred. They will be sure to pay doctors first for prevention, and then for successful cures, rather than for merely cycling as many patients through their offices as humanly possible.

In any situation where lifestyle choices can ameliorate health problems, those will be chosen in preference to endless medication. It does not cost the insurance company any money if you go for a walk or do some sit-ups; it does if you have to be on insulin for the rest of your life.

Conversely, medication is in general cheaper than surgery, all other things being equal, and so effective medications will be researched, developed and prescribed more often than invasive and dangerous surgery.

HEALTHCARE INFORMATION

Spending money on a pricey doctor is probably about the most cost-effective investment you will ever make. The most effective doctors are those who cure the most efficiently – and for sure, most customers of health care insurance would also purchase life insurance from the same company, so that any disastrously failed "cures" would cost the company an enormous amount of money.

In this way, returning a customer to health not only guarantees future health care payments, but it also postpones the payment of death benefits. In this way, the self-interest of the insurance company is directly aligned with the self-interest of the customer, who doubtless does not prefer to be either sick, or dead. If the doctor is also paid to prevent, cure and keep alive, then all three parties have the same goal, which is the polar opposite of any statist system.

Thus whenever anyone starts evaluating which health care insurance company to go with, each company would be tripping over themselves to provide independently verified statistics about the long-term health of their customers – the number of ailments prevented, identified and cured; the average life expectancy, successful pregnancies and births and so on. These companies would be selling *health* to you, rather than inflicting repetitive treatments on you, which is the case with socialized medicine.

The proactive and dedicated partnership between insurance company and customer – designed to serve the self-interest of each – would create a very positive and prevention-based healthcare approach. In the same way that companies that sell dental insurance require you to go for bi-annual checkups, proactive insurance companies would require regular health checkups. (I have experienced this directly in my career. Most investors require senior managers to be insured against illness, to protect their investment – in order to qualify for this, I had to go through a full checkup by a private agency, which reviewed my blood work, my history, and ran a wide battery of tests.)

In this way, the self-interest of the doctor – who normally gets paid for treatment, not cure – and that of the patient, who prefers prevention rather than treatment – can be productively aligned.

Health Care and the Poor

It is not a subject that many people are particularly comfortable with, but charity can be a very complex and dangerous thing.

We certainly want to help the unfortunate, but we do not wish to enable and subsidize bad decisions – this is only part of the complexity involved in helping others – which a statist society cannot distinguish or deal with at all.

If society gave everything that a poor person could possibly require in order to live comfortably, that would scarcely reduce the numbers of poor people, but would rather increase them considerably. On the other hand, the children of poor people are scarcely responsible for any bad decisions their parents may have made – however, if charities give a lot of money to poor people with children, more poor people will tend to have more children, which will only increase poverty.

This balancing act is one of the enormous and complex challenges of true charity – and yet *another* reason why a violent monopoly will never end up helping the poor in any substantive or permanent manner.

When it comes to health care, there is no doubt whatsoever that the majority of people care about the provision of health care for those who cannot afford it. At a hospital I visited recently, I saw a placard on the wall thanking the *five thousand* volunteers who helped run the place.

Doctors as a whole will always treat someone who comes with an immediate injury, whether they can pay or not. If we assume that medical treatments for the genuinely deserving and needy poor would consume about ten percent of general health care spending, then we can be completely certain that this amount of money would be donated by concerned individuals, either in time or money. We can be certain of this because we know of a large number of religious organizations that require ten percent of people's total income – twenty percent in fact, since this is pretax income – and people are quite happy to pay that.

Thus the medical needs of the poor would be entirely taken care of in a free society through charity and *pro bono* work. Charities would also compete to provide the most effective care for the poor, in order to gain the most donations. I would certainly prefer to give my money to an organization that was best able to create and provide sustainable health practices and medical treatments for the poor.

In this way, not only would the self-interest of doctors, insurance companies and customers be aligned – but also the self-interest of donators, charities and the poor they serve.

In a stateless society, the poor will be genuinely served by a far better system, composed of those whose self-interest is directly aligned with the health of the poor.

As has been shown over and over again, throughout history and across the world, benevolent self-interest, enhanced by free association and voluntary competition, is the only way to create sustainable compassion within society.

I am aware that I have not answered all possible objections to the question of how health care is provided in a free society. I am also aware that the possibility always exists that people can "fall through the cracks," or that charities could conceivably make mistakes, and either fund the wrong people, or fail to fund the right people.

Once more, this possibility of corruption and/or error is often considered to be an airtight argument against anarchy, when in fact it is an airtight argument *for* anarchy, and against statism.

Competition and voluntarism are the only known methodologies for repairing and opposing the inevitable errors and corruptions that constantly creep into human relations. The fact that human beings can make mistakes – and are always susceptible to corruption – is exactly *why* they should never be given a monopoly power of violence over others.

When an entrepreneur – whether charitable or for-profit – makes a mistake by failing to provide value – others will immediately rush in to provide the missing benefit.

It is this constant process of challenge and competition that allows the best solutions to be consistently discovered and reinvented in an ever-changing world.

STATELESS PRISONS

One of the great challenges of anarchistic philosophy is the problem of *prisons*, or the physical restraint of violent criminals. Let us examine the punitive mechanisms that might exist in the absence of a coercive State system.

Firstly, we can assume that in the absence of a State, DROs will necessarily band together to deny the advantages of a modern economic life to those individuals who egregiously harm their fellow citizens. Such necessities as bank accounts, credit, transportation, lodging, food and so on, can all be withheld from those who have been proven to have committed violent crimes. Also, in a stateless society, since there is no such thing as "public" property, violent criminals would have a tough time getting anywhere, since roads, parks, forests and so on would all be privately owned. Anybody providing aid or comfort to a person convicted of a violent crime could face a withdrawal of services and protections from their own DRO, and so would avoid giving such help.

However, this solution alone has not been sufficient for some people, who still feel that sociopathic and violent criminals need to be physically restrained or imprisoned for society to be safe.

Before tackling this issue, I would like to point out that if the problem of violent sociopaths is very extensive, then surely any moral justifications for the existence of a State become that much *more* untenable. If society literally *swarms* with evil people, then those evil people will surely overwhelm the State, the police, and the military, and prey upon legally disarmed citizens to their hearts content. If, however, there are very few evil people, then we surely do not need a State to protect us from such a tiny problem. In other words, if there are a lot of evil people, we cannot *have* a State – and if there are few evil people, then we do not *need* a State.

Also, whenever punitive measures are discussed, fears arise about unjust punishments. What if DROs act against someone who has been *wrongly* convicted of a crime? Well, according to our usual methodology, we must remember to compare a stateless society not to some perfect utopia, but rather to existing statist societies. Are people currently unjustly sent to prison? You bet. Are non-violent drug users jailed? Yes, by the millions. Do some people pretend to confess to less grievous crimes because they are threatened with terrifying sentences if they do not? Of course. Do the police manufacture evidence? Yes. Are policemen rewarded for preventing crimes, or obtaining convictions? The latter.

And – are war criminals such as George Bush charged with their genocidal crimes? Of course not. They are given pensions and speaking tours.

If we live in a terrifyingly obese nation, saying we should not bother dieting because some *thin* people get diabetes is irrational to say the least.

The Rapist

Let us imagine what might happen to a rapist in a stateless society. All general DRO contracts will include "rape protection," since DROs will want to avoid incurring the medical, psychological and income costs of a rape for one of their own customers. Part of "rape protection" will be the provision of significant financial restitution to a rape victim. (Women who can't afford "rape protection" will be subsidized by charities – or lawyers will represent them *pro bono* in return for a cut of the restitution.)

If a woman gets raped, she then applies to her DRO for restitution. The DRO then finds her rapist – using the most advanced forensic techniques available – and sends an agent to knock on his door.

"Good morning, sir," the agent will politely say. "You have been charged with rape, and I'm here to inform you of your options. We wish to make this process as painless and non-intrusive as possible for you, and so will schedule a trial at the time of your earliest convenience. If you do not attend this trial, or testify falsely, or attempt to flee, we shall apply significant sanctions against you, which are outlined in your existing DRO contract. Our agreement with your bank allows us to freeze your assets – except for basic living and legal expenses – the moment that you are charged with a violent crime. We also have agreements with airlines, road, bus and train companies, as well as gas stations, to prevent you from leaving town until this matter is resolved.

"You can represent yourself in this trial, choose from one of our lawyers, or we will pay for any lawyer you prefer, at standard rates. Also, as per our existing contract, we are to be allowed access to your home for purposes of investigation. You are free to deny us this access, of course, but then we shall assume that you are guilty of the crime, and will apply all the sanctions allowed to us by contract.

"If you are found to be innocent of this crime, we will pay you the sum of twenty thousand dollars, to be funded by the woman who has charged you with rape. We will also offer free psychological counseling for you, in order to help you avoid such accusers in the future."

The trial will commence, and will return a verdict in due course. (It seems highly likely that lie-detectors will be admissible, since they are more than 90% accurate when used correctly, which is better than most witnesses. The reason that they are not admissible now is that they would make lawyers less valuable, and also would reveal the degree to which the State police lie.)

If the man is found guilty, he will receive another visit from his DRO representative.

"Good afternoon, sir," the agent will say. "You have been found guilty of rape, and I'm here to inform you of your punishment. We have a reciprocal agreement with your bank, which has now put a hold on your accounts, and provided us limited access. We will be deducting double the costs of our investigation and trial from your funds, and will also be transferring half a million dollars to the woman that you raped. We are aware that you do not have sufficient funds to cover this cost, which we will address in a moment. We also have reciprocal agreements with the companies that provide water and electricity to your house, and those will now be cut off. Furthermore, no gas station will sell you gasoline, and no train station, airline or bus company will sell you a ticket. We have made arrangements with all of the local grocery stores to deny you service, either in person or online. If you set foot on the street outside your house, which is owned privately, you will be physically removed for trespassing. Your wife and children can leave at any time. If they have no place to go, we will cover their transition costs, and charge you for them.

"Of course, you have the right to appeal this sentence, and if you successfully appeal, we would transfer our costs to the woman who has accused you of rape, and pay you for the inconvenience we have caused you. If, however, your appeal fails, all additional costs will be added to your debt.

"I can tell you openly that if you choose to stay in your house, you will be unable to survive for very long. You will run out of food and water. You can attempt to escape your own house, of course, leaving all of your possessions. If you *do* successfully escape, be aware that you are now entered into a central registry, and no reputable DRO will ever represent you. Furthermore, all DROs which have reciprocal agreements with us – which is the vast majority of them – will withdraw services from their own customers if those customers provide you with *any* goods or services. For the rest of your life, it will be almost impossible for you to open a bank account, use centralized currency, carry a credit card, own a car, buy gas, use a road – or any other form of transportation – and gaining food, water and lodging will be a constant nightmare for you. You will spend your entire existence running, hiding and begging, and will never find peace, solace or comfort in any place.

"However, there is an option. If you come with me now, we will take you to a place of work for a period of ten years. During that time, you will be working for us in a capacity which will be determined by your skills. If you do not have any viable skills, we will train you. Your wages will go to us, and we will deduct the costs of your incarceration, as well as any of the costs I outlined above which are not covered by your existing funds. A small amount of your wages will be set aside to help get you started after your release.

"During your stay with us, we will do our utmost help you, because we do not want to have to go through all of this with again you in the future. You will take courses on ethics. You will take courses on anger management. You will take psychological counseling. You will emerge from your work term a far better person. And when you *do* emerge, all of your rights will be fully restored, and you will be able to participate once more in the economic and social life of society.

"You have a choice now, and I want you to understand the full ramifications of that choice. If you come with me now, this is the best offer that I can give you. If you decide to stay in your house, and later change your mind, the penalties will be far greater. If you escape, and later change your mind, the penalties will be greater still. In our experience, 99.99% of people who either run or stay end up changing their minds, and end up that much worse off. The remaining 0.01%? They commit suicide.

"The choice is now yours. Do the right thing. Do the wise thing. Come with me."

Can we really imagine that anyone would choose to stay in his own house and die of thirst, unable to even flush his toilet? Can we imagine that anyone would choose a life of perpetual running and hiding and begging? Even if the rapist had no interest in becoming a better person, surely the cost/benefit of the options outlined above would convince him.

There will always be a small number of truly evil or insane people within society. There are *far* better ways of dealing with them than our existing system of dehumanizing, brutal and destructive State gulags, which generally serve only to expand their criminal intent, skills and contacts. Also, it is important to remember that the existing State prisons contain relatively few evil or insane people. The majority of those in jail are nonviolent offenders, enslaved and in chains because they used recreational drugs, or gambled, or went to a prostitute, or did not pay all their taxes, or other such innocuous nonsense – or turned to crime because State "vice" prohibitions made crime so profitable, and State "education" kept them so ignorant.

Our choice, then, is between a system which removes the tiny minority of evil people from society, rehabilitates them if all possible, and makes them work productively to support their own confinement – or a State system which spends most of its time and energies enslaving innocent people, while letting the evil and insane roam free – or become Commander in Chief.

MONEY

Another central justification for the existence of the State is the need for a stable and universal monetary system. In the absence of any general system for determining price and value, the argument goes, economic activity grinds to a standstill, since all that is left in the absence of cash and prices is self-sufficiency, barter and/or an inefficient command economy of some kind.

If the government stops defining and promulgating the money supply, the argument goes, money would cease to exist, and the economy would collapse. Every group would come up with their own definition of money, and at the mall, you would have to try to negotiate with people who were using diamonds, gold, shark teeth, salt, spices, DVDs and goodness knows what else as cash.

Our economic life would thus become an endless runaround of attempting to match a variety of currencies to a variety of products; the value of our salaries would be diminished – or perhaps eliminated – by the amount of labor that it would take to find someone who would accept our "currency." Furthermore, given the enormous multiplicity of "currencies" in a stateless society, we would never be sure whether or not we were being ripped off in some manner, as someone tried to convince us that 12 shark's teeth were in fact equal to our bag of cinnamon – and horror of horrors, we might get home and find out that those shark's teeth were in fact fakes!

(I hope that we are far enough along in our understanding to recognize an "Argument from Apocalypse" when we see it!)

Like so many arguments against a stateless society, the above approach can be defined as the "idiot kindergarten" argument. In this view, society is composed of largely retarded adults, who find it impossible to cooperate for mutual advantage, but instead run around like chickens with their heads cut off, grabbing and snatching at whatever value they can, eyeing each other with suspicion and hostility, and probably eating glue and stuffing plasticine up their noses.

The essential thing to understand about money is that cash is just another product, exactly like an iPod, a car or a telephone line.

A telephone line is designed to facilitate communication in a "many to many" scenario – anyone who pays to access it can talk to anyone else who has paid to access it. From the standpoint of the consumer, a telephone line is an "invisible" medium for the exchange of conversation, from anyone, and to anyone.

In the same way, money is an "invisible" medium for the exchange of value in a market system. Money is only required because people wish to trade – I do not generally set a "market price" for the vegetables that I grow for my own consumption in my backyard. (Although my time certainly has a form of "price" of course…)

Money reflects the degree of *actionable* demand for goods and services – actionable because we all may want a Lamborghini, but very few of us actually have the money to purchase one.

Quite literally, money is a way of measuring apples versus oranges. How much of my economically productive time is a dozen oranges worth? How many oranges is a dozen apples worth? In the absence of money, the only alternative is direct trade, which is horribly inefficient, for the obvious reason that if I want to trade apples for oranges, I have to find someone who wants to trade oranges for apples.

Like any commodity, money has a price – and this price is called "interest." If I want to rent a car, rather than buy it, then I do not have to outlay the entire capital cost of the car, but rather I can borrow the car (which really means borrowing the capital cost of the car, since someone else has to have already paid for it) and pay a rental fee.

In the same way, if I want to borrow money, then I have to pay a "rental fee," which is *interest*, which equals the amount that I am willing to pay in order to have something sooner rather than later. "Interest" exists because *time* is the most precious commodity that we have, because it can never be replaced, and without it we are nothing.

I can save for 20 years in order to buy a house outright, but there is no particular value in that; it is true that if I take this approach, I have saved myself a loss of money and interest, but so what? I have only exchanged paying interest for paying rent on some other place to live – both of which are forms of non-recoverable income. Whether I hand my money to a bank or a landlord is immaterial.

If we are afraid that a stateless society will not be able to create or sustain any form of objective monetary system, then what we are really saying is that human beings will refuse to cooperate, even if their lack of cooperation means a complete collapse of the economic system, and the entire basis of their high living standard.

We can easily imagine that in the absence of cash, economic wealth and growth would collapse by probably 95%. Let us say that the average annual income of a developed economy is about $35,000 a year – when we reject a stateless society for fear that it cannot sustain a monetary system, we are really saying that human beings would accept an annual drop in income from $35,000 to $1,750 rather than cooperate with each other.

To put it another way, if I were willing to pay you $33,250 a year – the difference between living in a mud shack and living in a comfortable home, between near starvation and having more than enough food, between plumbing and an outhouse – in order to cooperate with other human beings, would you say "no"?

Of course not.

If human beings do not possess enough rational self-interest to accept a *20 fold* increase in their income simply for the sake of participating in some reasonable monetary system, then philosophy, medicine and society of any kind would be utterly impossible, and you would not be able to read this, because you would have said to yourself that the effort of learning how to read is not worth it.

I apologize if I am hammering the point perhaps too hard, but another way of understanding this is to imagine the following scenario.

THE ANARCHIST CREDIT CARD

Let us say that you make $35,000 a year, and one day, you get a letter in the mail from the Anarchist Credit Card Company:

Dear [You]:

*We have a very exciting offer for you! If you agree to sign up for the Anarchist Credit Card (ACC), and agree to use it for at least 80% of your consumer purchases, we will deposit **$700,000** into your ACC account every single year, free of charge, for you to spend as you see fit!*

We will also only charge you 1% interest per year...

Would that be an offer that just might interest you? $700,000 of free money every single year, just for signing up for and using particular credit card?

Well, this is exactly the anarchist offer!

Given the massive incentives involved in participating in a voluntary monetary system, we can be certain that all but the insane will leap at the opportunity.

Entrepreneurs who can offer people an immediate and permanent 20-fold increase in their income will not find any shortage of people willing to sign up for their services.

Thus, we can be absolutely and completely sure that a stateless society will have a stable and beneficial monetary system.

We can now spend some time examining how it might work.

WHAT PROBLEM ARE WE TRYING TO SOLVE?

It is always fascinating to see what Ayn Rand used to call the "blank out," which occurs when people defend the existing statist system of currency.

Government predation upon the economy through its monopoly on currency is one of the most savage and destructive aspects of a statist society.

The overprinting of money, which is used to bribe existing special interests, results in inflation, or the loss of purchasing power that results from too many dollars chasing too few goods and services.

If I wanted to start a credit card company, and sent out a business plan to investors informing them that my goal was to ensure that consumers paid 5% more per year for all their purchases, and use that as the basis for my profit, they would laugh at me as insane and ridiculous! "Who would sign up for such a vampiric credit card?" they would chortle, and probably send it around to each other as a joke.

Then, these very same investors will run across an anarchist, and end up defending the existing statist currency system, without even noticing the rank contradiction.

This is the true strangeness of the world that only the anarchist can see.

Inflation is a brutal attack upon the poor; deficit financing is also a staggering predation upon the unborn, the financial equivalent of a farmer securing a loan by pledging his unborn future livestock.

The reason that statist monetary systems always grow to collapse is the simple financial equation that lies at their root.

The reason that Mafia protection schemes "work" is because the costs of enforcement are far less than the rewards of intimidation. If you ask a restaurant owner for $1,000 a month in "protection," but it only costs you $100 a month to pay a thug to threaten him, the economic benefit is clear. In effect, the thug's wages are directly paid for by his victims, and the vast profits go to the thug's leaders.

The limitation in the profits of organized crime is the balance of power between the thugs and the restaurant owners. If the Mafia predation becomes too great, the owners will simply sell their restaurants and set up shop elsewhere. Alternatively, they can hire their own security guards to protect their restaurants, thus starving the Mafia out of business – or hire their own thugs to threaten the Mafia thugs in return. (In "The Godfather," for instance, a young Corleone decided to kill a thug rather than pay him.)

However, governments are subject to no such "restrictions." Moving out of Brooklyn is one thing; moving out of the United States is quite another, due to the time and expense involved. Furthermore, moving to another country does not solve the problem of taxation, because "protection money" will be violently extracted from you no matter where you end up living.

Furthermore, citizens cannot hire security guards to protect them against the police and the military, since they are so outgunned. Thus the limitations of evasion or retaliation simply do not exist in a statist society.

In addition, governments become less and less reliant on direct and immediate taxation over time, since their ability to print money and take out loans against future taxation diminishes the need to please the taxpayer in the short run.

Thus we can see that the Mafia would only continue to grow if they could somehow establish the following situations:

1. The restaurant owners could never leave.
2. The restaurant owners could never defend themselves.
3. The Mafia could take out legal loans against future "protection" profits.
4. The Mafia could print as much money as it wanted – whenever it wanted – and would never face any significant "counterfeit" competition.
5. The Mafia was well-paid to collect this protection money.

This situation would result in a cancerous growth in the size and power of the Mafia, because the significant imbalance between short-term gains and long-term pains would be so great that the deferral of immediate profits would never occur. We may as well expect a single and childless young man who knows that he has only two weeks to live to spend one of those weeks planning and investing in his retirement.

Of course, it is entirely natural and inevitable that the government defines its own actions as virtuous, and the *exact same actions* as evil and criminal if performed by others. Printing money is an essential and virtuous government function; the *private* printing of money is the evil act of "counterfeiting" – although both are the creation of fiat currency out of thin air for the private profiteering of particular individuals.

If you're in the mood for a bit of intellectual fun, it is always enjoyable to try out the following approach when arguing for an anarchist society: *describe how you think an anarchist society should run, but smuggle statist principles in, just to see if people notice the substitution.*

In the case of currency, I would say something like this:

"The way that I see currency working in a stateless society is that one particular private agency should have the right to print as much money as it wants, whenever it wants – and it should use this power to pay for an army that it would then use to shoot anyone who tried printing competing currencies. This agency should have the right to create debts for people who have not even been born yet, and to charge whatever it wants to the citizenry as a whole, using the future income that will steal from them as collateral for spending in the here and now!"

Naturally, people are shocked and appalled when I propose such a system. They consider it corrupt and evil for money to be created and promulgated in this manner, and immediately respond with myriad examples of the endless and immoral consequences of my proposed system.

Then, they inevitably defend the Federal Reserve...

The "shock treatment" of this sudden reversal has at least the potential to jolt someone's conscience into a kind of desperately-needed rationality, and help them finally see the savage amount of propaganda that has been inflicted on them.

Monetary Aspects of Stateless Money

It is impossible to know for certain how money will work in a stateless society, but I can at least tell you what *I* would prefer as a consumer.

Stability

One of the greatest – and unnecessary – challenges in existing statist societies is a near-complete inability to know what the future holds in terms of monetary stability. The interest rate goes up and down according to the whims of the leaders; more money is printed, and then less money is printed; the government scoops up more, then less, of available capital in terms of loans; bonds are issued with a variety of interest rates, and so on.

In particular industries, the business environment is even more random. Regulations swell and change; tariffs rise and alter; import restrictions grow and fall; union rules come and go – and the endless teasing possibility of government subsidies and contracts keeps many a faltering business around long after its natural expiry date.

Thus, the first guarantee that I would require from anyone wishing to enroll me in a monetary system would be *stability*. I do not want to have to worry about whether my money will be worth less next year, or whether its value is going to fluctuate in any substantial manner.

Portability

There is a reason that people tend to travel with credit cards, rather than with gift certificates for specific stores and restaurants. Since gift certificates are not as portable, they would have to carry a significant stack of them to spend money from place to place.

When traveling abroad, credit cards are generally preferable to cash, because they do not have to be converted, and are less convenient to steal.

In the same way, gold has been a common currency throughout history because it is rare, portable, strong enough to last (but soft enough to mould), universally valued, easily dividable, and does not lose value when it is split, like a diamond.

Thus, to get my business, any particular currency would have to offer *portability*.

The cost savings for monetary systems tend to take the form of a bell curve – when a currency is not very portable, like a gift certificate, it remains very cheap to produce and consume. When a currency becomes *somewhat* portable, it operates in a kind of limbo – it is much more expensive than a gift certificate, but not as cheap as a currency that is very portable, which has economies of scale working for it.

For instance, it might be valuable for the retailers in my geographical region to offer me a form of subsidized currency that I could only spend in their stores. This already occurs in used-books stores; you can either take cash or credit – and the credit is much more lucrative, because the store owner gains the additional value of knowing that you will buy only from him.

However, localized currencies face the significant disadvantage of being unusable in transactions that require wider economic reach. It is unlikely that the company that provides your electricity resides in your county, in which case your "local dollars" could not be used to pay your electricity bill, which would cost you additional time and energy to pay the bill from a different account, using a more universal currency.

In a stateless society, your bank could also analyze your spending habits and pro-actively buy particular currencies. If you spend $100 a month at Store X, it could buy 100 "Store X dollars" a month, getting a 5% discount, since Store X can book its un-spent consumer dollars as an asset and guarantee of future earnings. The bank may charge you 1% for this service, but you would still be 4% ahead.

We must remember that inconvenience breeds entrepreneurs. In a stateless so-ciety, an obvious service would be a "transparent" way of paying your bills using the most advantageous currency available. I might have bank accounts with five different kinds of currency – and thus my bank would provide bill payments in a universal for-mat; I would not need to know all the details, but the bank would complete my trans-action using the most advantageous currency. In this way, I might have different kinds of money, but that difference would be largely invisible to me, except for the savings I would receive. (Note that these different currencies would also be a disincentive for invasion, as mentioned above.)

Would it be cheaper for me to participate in a currency that would be accepted on the other side of the world? That is very hard to predict ahead of time, because there would be significant cost savings in a universal currency, but there would be significant costs as well. It is hard to imagine that a Chinese food seller would be inter-ested in offering currency-based discounts to a teenager in Zimbabwe, and so the local incentive to provide subsidized currency would be diminished. On the other hand, the significant amount of technical resources required to run any currency would not have to be duplicated.

Of course, since inconvenience breeds entrepreneurs, it is certain that a number of enterprising souls would come up with a framework for running currencies that could be populated with any number of specific currencies, just as websites almost never write their own "shopping cart" code from scratch, but rather populate existing frameworks with their own products and prices.

This approach could very easily overcome the problem of duplicate investments in technical currency frameworks – this, combined with a transparent abstraction layer for bill-paying in multiple currencies, would create an enormously efficient and user-friendly currency system – or systems, to be more precise.

Security

If the above two criteria were met, my next consumer question would be: *how secure is this currency?*

Security is always a delicate balance between usability and safety. Any online transaction could require you to enter 10 unique passwords, each 255 characters long, which would then be virtually unbreakable – the problem is that no one would use it, for the same reason that very few people put 20 locks on their front door, and walk around like some sort of apartment superintendent, their key rings clanking like a suit of chain mail. It certainly is an inconvenience to be robbed, but it is also inconvenient to spend 20 minutes opening and locking your door every day.

I would not require that my currency be perfectly secure (if this were even possible) – I would prefer that this security at least match my preferences and requirements.

Some people are carefree; some people are cautious, and some people are down-right paranoid. The paranoid people always prefer to shift the costs of securing their money to the carefree people; in the same way, the carefree people resent paying for all the extra security features that the paranoid prefer. Thus, any effective supplier of a monetary system would very likely have different levels of security and precautions, and would charge the appropriate costs for each level.

Carefree people might choose to have few if any security features at all, and thus pay the least for participating in a monetary system. On the other hand, the paranoid might require voice and fingerprint identification, as well as retina scans, specific dance moves and obscure Urdu phrases in order to complete a transaction. All this specialization is part and parcel of the inevitable entrepreneurial obsession with providing the most possible value in every conceivable situation, in order to avoid leaving even one thin dime of potential profit on the table.

Of course, a central purpose of the free market is not to create profit, but rather to eliminate it, or at least make it as small as possible. Any firm which overcharges will inevitably be undercut, which is why profits even in successful companies are generally no more than a few percentage points. Thus we can be sure that there will be just the right number of currency systems in a free society – not so many that economic interactions become complicated and cumbersome, but not so few that a lack of competition will allow profits to inflate.

The majority of economic transactions in a free society will be performed electronically, because the transaction costs are far lower – however, cash will always be necessary, for a variety of reasons. The price of cash transactions, being higher, will be reflected in a lack of discounts – or a surcharge – in the price, which will discourage but not eliminate these kinds of interactions. It also seems likely that cash will not carry a guarantee of restitution in the case of loss or theft, in the way that electronic currency would, unless there was a way to electronically associate cash with a particular individual.

At the moment, it may seem that electronic transactions are subjected to a surcharge, while cash transactions are not – however, this is not the case at all.

Credit card companies do charge a few percentage points per transaction, while cash can get you certain kinds of discounts at computer stores, but in reality the exact reverse is true.

Currently, if you take your money and put it under a mattress, it will lose a few percentage points at least per year due to inflation. Furthermore, a certain percentage of your taxes is used to maintain and defend the statist monopoly on currency. It is quite likely – if we include debts and deficits – that you are paying at least 10% of your income for the "privilege" of participating in a statist currency system. This system has all the characteristics of any brutal and violent monopoly, which is that it is exploitive, random, destructive, cancerous, and on a certain course toward annihilation.

I pay a percentage point or two on most of the donations I receive for Freedomain Radio, which come through PayPal. I assume that in a free market, this would be halved at least – thus I think it is safe to say that currency transactions would be very likely around 1% of the total value, or one tenth of the bare minimum of what you're paying at the moment for the statist system.

A 90% reduction in cost, combined with far greater security features, guaranteed stability in the value of the currency, portability proportional to your requirement – as well as discount incentives to shop in particular areas – would result in an essentially "free" monetary system. (It would also doubtless be the case that you could choose not to pay a penny in fees to use a currency, if you were willing to submit to advertisements on that currency!)

Bankruptcy?
What would happen, though, if a particular currency DRO ended up going bankrupt? Would everyone end up losing his or her life savings?

The standard cliché here – at least for older people – is the "bank run" scene in Depression-era movies, where frantic people storm a bank desperate to get their money, once they hear that it might be going out of business.

Of course, this vision is always considered to be negative towards banks, rather than towards the relatively new Federal Reserve, which was in charge of the currency for the entire nation. In the same way, if a foreign enemy were to bomb farm fields in the Midwest, it is doubtless the greedy capitalist grocery store owners who would be blamed and vilified in perpetuity for the resulting price increases.

Let us say that some greedy or improvident DRO currency provider started running his company poorly – what would happen?

Well, the first thing that would happen is that his investors and board of directors would notice.

The first thing that I would require from the group in charge of any currency system I was involved in would be that they hold the majority of their savings in the currency system that they are trying to sell to me. I would demand external audits to ensure that at least 80% of their savings were in their own currency system. The moment that any of these people began to sell off their own currency holdings, it would be a clear indication that they no longer had faith in the long-term viability of what they were selling.

Secondly, I would require an immediate sale of the company should its asset/debt ratio exceed a very conservative number. How would a sale help me? Well, if someone wanted to buy a distressed currency company, he or she would only want to do so if the existing customer base could be retained. In other words, additional benefits would have to be offered to the customers in order to retain them – a fee holiday, some sort of cash bonus or something like that. In order to keep me from withdrawing my money from this currency system, someone would have to pay me to accept the increased risk if it was in distress.

Thirdly, I would demand that any significant losses come directly out of the bank accounts and assets of those in charge of the currency. If I ended up only being paid 80 cents on the dollar, because they had screwed up the business, I would make damn sure that they ended up with zero cents on the dollar, and living in a van down by the river as well!

This would eliminate the incentive for managers to prey upon the company for personal gain. No matter how badly their customers ended up, they would end up in a far worse situation.

Fourthly, I would demand the right to withdraw all of my money at any time I wanted.

Let us now trace the likely sequence of events that would occur if a currency company got into financial trouble.

As mentioned above, the leadership and investors would be very quickly aware of any potential problem, and would be equally if not painfully aware that if a whiff of scandal or instability leaked into the marketplace, their entire investment may very well go down the drain.

Since voluntarism and a free society is all about preventing problems, rather than curing them – the direct opposite of statism, which is all about inventing problems, and then exacerbating them – managers and investors would be hyper-vigilant in protecting the financial soundness of their organization. The success of any voluntary money system starts and ends with credibility and trust – the moment that either becomes even remotely compromised, the entire system is called into question. Competitors will always be looking for weaknesses in other monetary systems, and will provide incentives to lure customers away. Thus the investors and managers would put every conceivable check and balance in place to ensure that the system remained trustworthy.

Should some upcoming problem escape them, however, and Company XYZ were to encounter real financial difficulties, what would happen?

Well, when any company hits a financial problem, it is either because it is no longer viable, or it is being badly run. Since we have already established the innate value of and requirement for currency, we know that XYZ cannot be in trouble because no one needs its services anymore – thus its difficulties must result from being badly run.

If a company is being badly run, it can either reform itself from within, or it cannot.

If XYZ *can* reform its management practices from within, then bankruptcy will not be the result of its misstep – some firings, some dropped bonuses, and some cutbacks, but not bankruptcy. Customers might not even have a clear sense that anything is amiss at all.

Ah, but what happens if XYZ *cannot* reform itself from within?

In any free market system, there exists a plethora of so-called "raiders" who are constantly looking for poorly-run companies to snap up and improve. These raiders would doubtless very quickly sniff out the problems within the company, and would try to take it over in some manner.

If I were one of these raiders, I would face a very difficult balancing act, which is that it would be advantageous for me to leak the problems XYZ was experiencing, in order to drive down the value of the company and pick it up for less money – however, such a leak would also create a panic among the customers, which could largely eliminate the value of the company.

Thus, my best strategy would be to leak the problems at XYZ – and simultaneously offer a guarantee to existing customers that their currency would be protected, as well as some sort of incentive or bonus to retain their allegiance. I would be willing to put all of this in writing, of course, in a binding contract, which would take effect the moment I got control of the company.

This would cause a temporary dip in the price of XYZ, thus allowing me to gain control of it more cheaply – and would at least help alleviate the fears of existing customers by providing a binding guarantee to retain the value of their money.

However, as a raider, I would be facing significant competition from another source – other currency companies.

Company ABC, on hearing about any possible problems with XYZ, would immediately take out full-page advertisements, offering significant bonuses to any XYZ customers who transferred their money to the ABC Company. There would be so many "lifeboat" companies offering to rescue XYZ customers at par or greater that such customers would doubtless be able to walk to shore!

It could be the case that whatever solution any individual customer chooses might not pan out – in other words, a raider might offer a five percent bonus to currency holdings, and then fail to deliver it, falter in his execution, and customers might end up having to pull out at eighty or ninety cents on the dollar.

Color me cold, but I cannot see the innate tragedy in such a situation. Anyone who offers you "free" money does so with the implicit – though perhaps unspoken – background of risk. If I decide to leave my money in a troubled company, in the hopes of gaining five percent more, and I end up getting ten percent less, it is hard to see how that is significantly different from investing in a stock or a bond – or a horse, for that matter.

Thus, there is no conceivable situation in which currency customers would wake up one day to find their savings utterly wiped out – there is so much profit in customer retention, particularly in currency situations, that a literal stampede of entrepreneurs would attempt to insert themselves into the equation, to the benefit of the existing customers.

Compared to What?

Doubtless there are ten thousand churning minds out there at this very moment, chanting their heated way through every conceivable possibility that might result in financial ruin for customers of the XYZ Currency Company. And perhaps such a possibility exists – but again, this is an argument *for* anarchism, not *against* it.

Any farmer can fail to produce crops at any particular time – this is a natural reality and risk of farming, or indeed of any human endeavor.

Since any farmer can fail to produce crops, the only way that we can guarantee – as best as possible – the continual supply of crops is to have a large number of farmers. If we only have one farmer for the entire world – to take an exaggerated example – then the moment that the inevitable happens, and that farmer fails to produce crops, worldwide starvation inevitably results.

This distribution of risk is an essential part of any rational strategy to reduce danger. If you are only ever allowed to buy one stock your whole life long, then you may do very well, but you also may do very badly. Diversification is the key to minimizing risk.

In the same way, when we have a State monopoly on currency, and we accept that currency organizations can fail from time to time – and certainly there is no shortage in history of examples of States corrupting and destroying their currencies – we have truly all of our eggs in one very precarious basket.

If we are truly concerned about currency failure in a free market system, then the worst possible solution we could come up with would be to create a violent monopoly over a single currency. If we are concerned about farm failures, then obviously the solution is to have as many farms as economically possible, so that those that fail can be shored up by those that succeed.

In other words, if currency failure is *not* a problem, then a stateless society is the best solution.

If currency failure *is* a problem – then a stateless society is the best solution.

SAVING CHILDREN: THE STATELESS SOCIETY AND THE PROTECTION OF THE HELPLESS

All moralists interested in improving society must answer the most essential questions about human motivation, and show how their proposed solutions will create a rational framework of incentives, punishments and rewards that further moral goals generally accepted as good. The 20th century clearly showed that there is no possibility for ideology to invent or create an "ideal man" – and that all such attempts generally create a hell on earth. Utopian thinkers must work with man as he is, and recognize the inevitability of self-interest and the positive responses to incentives that characterize the human soul.

In the previous chapters on the stateless society, I have shown how society can operate in the absence of a centralized government. One question that repeatedly arises in response to these possibilities has been the following:

In the absence of a centralized State-run police force and law/court system, how can child abuse be prevented, or at least minimized?

When discussing ethical issues, it is essential to deal with what is arguably the greatest evil within human society: the abuse of children by their parents or primary caregivers. If we can create a society that treats children better than they are currently treated, we have created a goal or a destination worthy of the considerable efforts it will take to achieve it.

In any post-tribal society, family life generally becomes very opaque. Great evils can be committed within the family home, in isolation from the general view of society, and children by their very nature can do almost nothing to protect themselves. Excepting grave or obvious physical injuries, governmental agencies rarely get involved – and even when such agencies *do* get involved, it is far from clear that their involvement results in a better situation for the victimized child.

As we know from totalitarian regimes, any situation which combines an extreme disparity in authority with a lack of accountability for those in power tends to increase abuse. This does not mean that all parents are abusive, of course, but it does mean that in situations where abusive tendencies *do* exist, the power differential between parents and children, combined with the reality that few parents face any legal or direct financial consequences for their abuse, tends to prolong and exacerbate child maltreatment.

Due to this situation, it is hard to say that the existing system works to maximize the protection and security of children. While there is no perfect utopia wherein all children will be loved, nurtured and protected, any society which contains strong positive incentives for good parenting is a vast improvement over the current situation. Since children are by far the most vulnerable members of society, if a stateless society can protect them better than a statist society, it is perhaps the greatest moral benefit that anarchism can bring to bear on the human condition.

Before discussing how a stateless society can far better protect children, let us first look at how existing societies create problems for children.

- The existence of the welfare state has directly contributed to the rise of single-parent families. Abuse is generally more prevalent in single-parent families.
- The war on drugs has created extremely unstable, volatile and violent social circumstances.
- Government-run housing projects have gathered together unstable single mothers and unstable drug dealers (in fact, housing projects are sometimes called "girlfriend farms" for such men) – thus exposing children to highly dysfunctional role models.
- Public school education often creates unstable and dangerous environments for children, where younger children in particular are easy prey for bullies.
- The rise of taxation has reduced take-home income to the point where, for many families, both parents need to work. This has left children vulnerable to abuse by outside caregivers – and often leads to an excess of unsupervised time for children in their early teens.
- Government-run social agencies are no better at protecting children than any other State agencies are at protecting the environment, helping the poor, healing the sick, or any of the other self-appointed "missions" that bureaucrats devise for themselves.
- If a badly-raised child becomes a criminal, parents are not directly liable for the resulting social, medical, legal or property costs.
- If, through their bad parenting, parents end up alienating their children, they face far fewer financial problems in their old age, due to State-run social security benefits.

It is clear, then, that the existing system has room for improvement, let us say. How, then, does a stateless society better encourage good parenting?

First of all, in a stateless society, disputes between people are mediated by DROs. Is there any way that DROs can profitably intervene in a situation where there are deteriorating relationships between parent and child, or where the child is being directly harmed?

One of the primary reasons for the existence of DROs is to protect citizens against unacceptable levels of risk. In a free society, if a child goes off the rails and begins hurting other people or damaging their property, DROs will hold the parents responsible. To take a true disaster scenario, if your child paralyzes another child, you as a parent will be on the hook for a lifetime of medical bills, rehabilitation and equipment. Given that childhood – even in the absence of malice – is a physically risky time, few parents would accept the risk of having no protection for any potential injuries their child might commit or experience.

Like any insurance company, DROs would lower rates for children who were less at risk. An insurance company would prefer that your child be active – or they would face the health problems which naturally arise from inactivity – but not that your child be aggressive, especially towards other children. Children who learned positive negotiation skills – or at least did not hit, throw, punch or push other children – would be cheaper to insure. Parents who raised aggressive children would be charged far more in insurance than those who raise more peaceful offspring.

Some forms of child abuse do not generally result in destructive tendencies towards others, but rather towards the self. Anorexia nervosa, self-mutilation, excessive piercings and hyper-dangerous activities are all signs that a child has experienced specific forms of abuse – usually sexual in nature. Given that DROs also provide health insurance, it seems likely that DROs would do as much as possible to prevent and detect these kinds of activities, since they scarcely profit from self-destructive behavior.

At this point, you may be thinking that bad parents would scarcely stay in a DRO system, since it would be very expensive to insure their children. This is a natural response, but incorrect.

For instance, most parents prefer to have their children educated – even parents who abuse their children. Most schools would doubtless prefer DRO coverage for their students, because "unprotected" children would be more risky to have around. Thus, in order to get their children educated, parents have to have a DRO contract that protects them. If you are a bad parent, it will be almost impossible to avoid the significant costs imposed upon you.

Furthermore, I would prefer that my DRO refuse to insure parents without also insuring their children, because I care deeply about the health and well-being of children.

I am sure that I am not alone in this desire.

PROACTIVE PROTECTION

Currently, when you apply for medical insurance in the United States, you are subjected to a battery of tests aimed at determining your general level of health, and so your future medical risks. Similarly, life insurance costs usually depend on health indicators such as smoking, blood pressure and cholesterol levels. Also, the earlier that you buy insurance, the lower your initial payments are.

Thus, we can imagine that a variety of DROs will approach new parents with a number of different insurance offers, all designed to protect their children.

These DROs will be eager to offer the lowest possible rates for the parents. How can they achieve that? When a young man applies for his first car insurance, the insurance company usually takes into account any driving courses that he has taken. Similarly, DROs will offer lower rates to parents who take specific training on how to best raise children to be peaceful, safe and healthy members of society. DROs will also work hard to determine exactly which parenting practices are most likely to produce such happy children.

Children need very specific guidelines and parenting skills at different stages in their development. Given that parents are likely to want to keep insurance coverage on their children until they turn 18 – and that DROs are very interested in preventing problems over the long run – it also seems likely that DROs will continue to provide lower-cost coverage if parents update their parenting skills periodically.

There are other significant indicators that parenting is becoming problematic. For instance, parental substance abuse virtually guarantees that the children will be abused or neglected. DROs will offer far lower rates to parents who have either never shown these tendencies, or if they have, are willing to subject themselves to rehabilitation and random testing to prove that they are still clean. Remember that these tests are in no way intrusive in nature – parents can always refuse to take such tests, and simply accept the consequences.

What about the children? Since prevention is by far the better part of cure, their insurance costs will remain the lowest if potential problems can be identified before they manifest themselves in costly antisocial behavior. With the young in particular, early intervention is the key. How can DROs best keep the costs low for these children? Intermittent psychological and behavioural assessments would be a good start, as would proactive parenting classes. Naturally, no parents would ever be required to submit their children for assessment – they would just pay for the increased costs if they did not.

If a child displayed truly problematic behavior, DROs would threaten to drop family coverage entirely unless the parents accepted intervention.

This combination of research, financial incentives and constant updating creates three partners in the raising of children – parents who wish to keep their children happy and their insurance costs as low as possible, DROs who wish to prevent problems rather than pay for their remediation, and experts who constantly research and communicate best practices in parenting.

Parents who were themselves poorly raised often do not understand the best way to raise their own children. Lacking access to objective information and best practices, they often repeat the same mistakes that were inflicted upon them. Parents currently reluctant to "lift the blinds" on their parenting and familial circumstances would be presented with strong and positive financial incentives to do so. Parents who refused any kind of DRO coverage for their children – or who refused reasonable interventions to help them improve their parenting – would face negative repercussions from the DRO system, which have been discussed at length above. Thus it seems highly likely that a stateless society would create a wide variety of social interests all focused on improving the parenting of children, and ensuring the children were raised to be as peaceful, happy and productive as possible.

A Parenting Fable

There is an old fable that goes something like this: the Sun and the Wind are having an argument as to which one of them is stronger. The Wind boasts that he is able to uproot trees, tear the roofs off houses and throw down power lines. The Sun looks sceptical. Below them, as they argue, a man is walking along a country road. "Ah", says the Wind, "I bet I can tear the cloak right off this man's back!" "Go ahead," smiles the Sun. The Wind goes down and tears around this man, attempting to pry his cloak off his back. Naturally, the man simply clutches his cloak tighter, and the Wind can find no purchase. Finally, exhausted, the Wind withdraws. "Let me show you how it's done," says the Sun. Bursting into full brilliance, the Sun generates enormous heat, and the man begins to sweat. After ten minutes or so, the man sighs, wipes his brow – and slowly shrugs off his cloak.

This parable contains a powerful message about the difference between a stateless society, and society ruled by centralized government. The government always tries to force people to do things, which only increases their resistance and secrecy with regard to State power. Human society, though, only advances when a multiplicity of competing voluntary agencies create and maintain circumstances which truly benefit virtue and punish vice. This is an apt description of the free market – and it is also a description of the manner in which a stateless society will continually work to improve the safety and happiness of children.

PREVENTING TRAGEDY – AN ANARCHIC ANALYSIS OF ABORTION

Abortion is always a tragedy, and one of the saddest occurrences on this earth. Government "solutions" are also *always* disastrous, and so it is hard to understand how combining a tragedy with a disaster can create any kind of positive outcome. Mixing arsenic with mercury does not solve the problem of poison – and combining the violent inefficiency of the State with the tragedy of abortion does not solve the problem of family planning.

All those wishing to reduce the incidence of abortion – surely all rational and sensitive souls – must recognize that giving the government the power to combat abortion also gives it the power to *promote* abortion, which it currently does to a hideous degree. The best way to reduce the incidence of abortion is to withdraw State subsidies and allow the economic and social consequences to accrue to those who engage in sexually risky behaviours.

Reducing the incidence of abortion is not very complicated, since it is subject to the same laws of supply and demand as any other human activity. Simply put, any activity that is subsidized will increase, and any activity that is taxed will decrease. The incidence of abortion will go down only when abortion is no longer subsidized – and when responsible family planning is no longer taxed.

Abortion is very rare in a stable marriage, and is generally only performed under an extremity of financial or medical distress. The vast majority of abortions occur to single women, or women in unstable relationships. Particularly over the past fifty-odd years, the role of sexuality has been forcibly separated from marriage and procreation.

This is an entirely predictable – although perfectly horrible – development, given the role of the State in breaking down stable family structures.

Subsidizing Abortion

In general, any program which subsidizes pregnancy in the absence of a stable family structure will also tend to encourage abortion. In particular, State subsidies which encourage the pursuit of sexual pleasure in the absence of virtue, financial stability (or at least opportunity) and personal responsibility will also tend to increase the number of abortions. When the financial and social consequences of pregnancy are mitigated through State programs, risky sexual behaviours will inevitably increase – resulting in an increase of both pregnancies and abortions.

Controlling or mitigating the financial consequences of unwanted pregnancies directly alters the kinds of decisions that women make about sexual practices and partners. Having a child out of wedlock is one of the most costly decisions a woman can make, insofar as it tends to significantly arrest her educational, emotional and career development. The physical impossibility of being able to work for money and care for an infant at the same time reduces most young single mothers to a life of dependency, exhaustion and poverty. The chance of meeting a good man when already burdened with a baby lowers a single mother's chances for a good marriage. Not only does she come with a baby and significant expenses, but she probably also has few economic skills to offer. Plus, it is hard to date when you are breastfeeding. For these and many other reasons, single mothers often end up settling for unstable, unreliable men, just to have any sort of man around. Inevitably, the chances of having another baby thus increase – sadly, without a corresponding increase in relational stability.

This is why, in the past, society expended considerable effort to ensure that women did not get pregnant before marriage. The staggering financial losses incurred by childbirth without commitment usually accrued to the new grandparents, and so it was those parents who tried to do their best to prevent such a disaster. This need, being common to all parents, was generally shared across society, creating a near-impenetrable web of sexual chaperoning. (Social self-government based on individual incentives is the only way that social problems have been – or ever will be – solved to any degree of stability.)

It currently costs about $250,000 to bring a child from birth to age 18, under the current system. In a free market environment, with fully privatized and charity-supported education, health care, housing and so on, this cost will decrease of course (since all taxation would cease, and competition increase) – but it would still be considerable.

Babies, in short, are expensive. However, when the welfare state enters the equation, all of the above changes. Now, if a young woman gets pregnant out of wedlock, she can survive quite nicely. She will very likely never be rich – or probably even middle class – but she will be able to survive on some combination of any of the hundreds of State subsidies which directly benefit poor mothers.

In addition to the usual suspects – welfare, Medicare, child supplements, food stamps – there are many other ways she can lean on the State. When her child grows up, the State will also pay for his or her education. Does she need to take the bus? That is subsidized as well. Drop her child off for a story at the library? Subsidized. Daycare is subsidized as well, as is her apartment through rent control or public housing. Dental problems? No problem – subsidies take care of most if not all of the bills. The amount of money and resources provided to single mothers by the State is literally staggering! And when she gets old? Not to worry if she has been unable to save much money, or has alienated her children – Social Security will take care of her!

Since getting pregnant while unmarried is no longer a "life or death" issue, a young woman has far less incentive to keep her womb to herself until the right man comes along. She will not have a great life economically, but she will survive just fine – and also nicely avoid having to slave away at low-rent jobs. If you were staring at years of McJobs before you got any kind of decent career, "Plan B for Baby" might start looking pretty attractive, too!

Through such State-enforced subsidies, young women are seduced into self-destructive decisions, and sink into an underworld of dependent and dangerous lifestyles. If they have daughters, those girls will grow up in a world filled with unstable men, and without a loyal father's love and guidance. What are the odds of such girls growing up to be sexually responsible? Not nil, certainly, but not high either.

As a result of the increasing subsidization of poor sexual choices, the stage is set for rising numbers of abortions – and, since having an unnecessary abortion is one of the most egregious examples of preferring short-term gains to long-term gains, subsidizing error is scarcely the best method of encouraging greater rationality.

Taxing Family Planning

It is very hard to make good decisions when everyone around you is making bad decisions. Either you go along, and jump right into their pit of error, or you withdraw, provoking social ostracism and, all too often, outright hostility. When, encouraged by the endless subsidies of State programs, a certain number of unplanned pregnancies are reached, they become the norm, and vaguely something "not to be criticized." Young women, in order to keep their friends and not be attacked as "superior," often decide that it is cool to engage in sexually risky activities. When combined with the financial incentives outlined above, the "social acceptance" motive proves overwhelming for far too many women.

What alternatives are available to those young women who decide to take the "straight and narrow" course and avoid risky behaviours? What kind of opportunities are out there? Minimum wages, State-monopoly unions, over-regulation, crippling taxation, mind-numbing apprenticeship programs and a thousand other political factors have virtually killed off good job opportunities for the poor and unskilled. Jobs are scarce, taxes are high, and careers almost impossible. State schools fail to train poor youngsters for anything useful, and higher education is probably out of the picture as well. So it is fairly safe to say that productive and honorable lifestyles are as thwarted as irresponsibility and instant gratification are encouraged.

The Men

So far we have only been talking about women – but what about the men? How has male behaviour been affected by these fundamental reversals in social values? Well, as the negative effects of sexual indiscretion become smaller and smaller, men also become conditioned to expect, let us say, "short term" interactions with the fairer sex. As more and more women decide to engage in risky sex without requiring a commitment, the value of education, integrity and hard work for men goes down proportionally. As male virtue becomes debased, other values, more sinister and shallow, take their place. Women go for "hot" guys, or guys with lots of cash to spend, or with the kind of predatory status that comes with gang membership. The entire ecosystem of sexual attraction and stable provision is turned upside down, and the men formerly viewed as losers become winners – and vice versa.

Thus, a woman looking for a "good" man faces a distinct scarcity of such paragons – and may also face the mockery of her peers if she chooses a geeky provider over a shifty stud-muffin. "Good men" become more scarce – and objects of ridicule to boot. Female attractiveness, formerly the coin that purchased male loyalty, now becomes a magnet for shallow and unstable man-boys looking for another notch in their belts.

Problems such as abortion are so complex that they cannot be solved without reference to the shifting nature of rewards and punishments created by an ever-growing and ever-violent State. Like most social problems, the solution must be voluntary, and based on the financial, social and moral realities of biology and economics.

PART 4

Conclusions

• • •

The Value of Anarchism

I AM OFTEN ASKED WHY on earth anyone should get interested in anarchism, when there is virtually no chance that a stateless society will ever come into existence in our lifetime, or in the foreseeable future at all.

This is a very interesting question, and to some degree it involves a very personal answer, and so I hope you will forgive me if I forego the odd syllogism or two, and speak directly from the heart.

The Future

The story of the progress of human morals is almost entirely populated by people who did not live to see the world that they loved in their minds. Those to whom the idea of the separation of church and state arose as a tiny, faint glimmer over the burning horizon of religious warfare did not live to see these two whores pried apart by the power of philosophy.

Those who first dreamed of a world free of slavery lived only to see slavery increase and worsen, not diminish and collapse.

Those who dreamed of reason, evidence and science in the late Middle Ages saw their dreams go up in endless flames – and, all too often, themselves as well, under the burning mercies of Christian "salvation."

Those who dream of peaceful debate rather than flashing swords taste the bitter dregs of hemlock, not the sweet nectar of victory.

It is an inevitable consequence of inertia and corruption that those who dream of a better world almost always die before those dreams come true. The entrenched and pompous self-righteousness of viciousness and exploitation always moves to discredit any attack with all the resources it has stolen. The embedded corruptions of existing familial, professional, economic and political relationships is a sinewy Hydra that a thousand men with a thousand swords cannot possibly bring down in one generation.

However, you may say, even if this is true, what form of altruistic madness could take hold of us to the point where we are willing to sacrifice so many comforts in this world in order to secure a better one for people we shall never meet? Why should I care for people who are living 200 years from now, and their opinion of me, and those who fight beside me in a war whose spoils only the unborn will receive? Even if they thank us, and build statues in our names, what possible good can that do for us now? Why should we give up all the creature comforts of blind conformity and refuse to surrender to the endless momentum of the cultural riptide, gaining no love and peace in the present, but rather only willed incomprehension and spiteful calumny?

There may be those among us who are motivated for the most part by a love for a future that they shall never inhabit. There may be those of us willing to sit in the dark and tell tales of green fields to our fellow dungeon-dwellers, so that our grandchildren's children, whose lineage has been sustained by the bright stories of a free world beyond their walls, can emerge from the rubble of their crumbling jails into a sunlight that has been pictured and predicted, though not seen, for many decades.

And it *will* be our world, this world of the future, that we shall never tread. The evils and pettiness of the world that is will fall away from our rising ideals, like unneeded past boosters from a rocket piercing the stratosphere and launching to the stars. The door to this world of beauty, and plenty, and generosity, and peace, and benevolence can only be opened by the key of philosophy, of wisdom. I personally consider it the greatest possible honor to do my part in helping to fashion this golden key. I am a kind of intransigent warrior, far more at home in this time of war, the war for the future, than I would be I think in this world of the future, where all major foes and evils have been laid to rest. A natural warrior can rejoice to be born in a time of war – I am just such a born fighter, and take enormous pride and satisfaction in confronting and attempting to master the embedded evils and lies of the human mind. The size of my soul, it has turned out, is directly proportional to the size of my enemies, the enemies of wisdom and virtue. In this time, where the exploration of this world has largely ceased, but the exploration of other worlds has yet to begin, my restless, combative and explorative nature finds its true natural home and greatest possible purpose in the mental wrestling with unseen demons.

Thus, I can genuinely say that I could not conceivably wish to be born or to live in any other time. This new universe of instantaneous communication is my natural element, and the endless potential of these unexplored lands of thoughts, feelings, dreams and insights has given my soul scope to expand in a way that I never imagined possible. I am hopefully slightly larger than the size of my enemies; and certainly far smaller than the scope of the world I explore.

For me, then, the small pleasures of social conformity shrink to insignificance next to the glory of leading the charge in this kind of battle, the thrill of reasoning out new connections, the excitement of lighting up my own mind, and helping to light up the minds of others. To feel the power of significant evolution within the span of a few years, within my own mind, within my own soul, within my own life, is for me a staggering and unprecedented gift, which I would live a thousand years of social discomfort in order to attain.

I am also acutely aware of the reality that had I been born and lived in a different time – a later time, or an earlier one – I would have been pedaling a bicycle with a broken chain, if you understand me. The power of the conversation that I have initiated and am involved in is what gives my mind traction, links and engages it in the real world; it is the other stick that brings the new fire.

Thus for me it is an irreplaceable privilege to be doing what I am, where I am, during this time in history. I am a man who is excited by navigation, not the unloading of cargo. I live to explore, not to settle and consolidate. I live for battle, not administration.

I fully realize that my joys are not everyone's joys. If you do not happen to have my particular fetish for the endless swordplay of abstract battles, why on earth would you be interested in exploring and understanding the characteristics of a land you will never set foot on?

Anarchy and Relationships

Within our minds, because of our personal histories, there exists – for want of a better phrase – a kind of "dead zone," which is the black and broken scar tissue of the endless dictatorial commandments we were subjected to as children.

These commandments may have existed within your own home, but without a doubt this is exactly what you were subjected to in school. When you were a young child, opening up and exploring your own mind, and the new world before you, your teachers – and by proxy, your parents – never asked you what you most wanted to learn and explore.

Instead, you were jammed into a little desk, in a tight boxlike row with other children, while a teacher scratched with grating chalk on an old blackboard. Your individuality was not respected and explored; the natural and specific direction of your mind was not harnessed and expanded; your latent talents and abilities were not teased and conjured into full, magnificent view.

This was a dictatorial, almost entirely one-sided "relationship" – and this "relationship" showed up in school, in church, and very likely at home as well. Who really *cared* what you thought? Who really cared what you preferred to do? Were you not in general treated, at home, in school and at church, as a generally disobedient and largely inconvenient kind of pet? Did people talk to you, ask you questions, sit down and open you up to yourself – or did they feed you, clothe you, wash you and *manage* you? Was your childhood a more or less endless series of little commandments and "suggestions" – put that down, pick that up, don't go there, go here, share, be nice, don't raise your voice, go and read a book, turn that off, brush your teeth, finish your homework, don't use those words, use these words, stop playacting, calm down, go to bed, wake up – all of these teeth-gritting and petty commandments circle your childhood like an endless buzzing cloud of little gnats, that can never be swatted, are never full, and can never be escaped.

In the face of the needs and preferences of others – particularly those in authority – do we not fall back on a kind of empty, dull and resentful conformity? When others get irritated with us – particularly in our personal relationships – do we not either flash up with resentment, or sink back with resentment? Do we not either bully back, or surrender and plot?

When we explore anarchy as a theoretical ideal, we slowly and surely – and painfully – make gradual inroads back into this "dead zone." Like the last man in a city struggling to start the generator that will bring it back to life, when we continually re-imagine what it is like to sit on the other side of that negotiating table, we re-grow these deadened nerve endings of resentful conformity and dull compliance.

In the statist paradigm, we listen only to God, and obey His commandments.

In the anarchist paradigm, God also listens to us, and we negotiate as equals.

When we mentally practice sitting on the other side of that negotiating table, we re-learn a lesson that has long been pounded out of us – the lesson of empathy and mutually-advantageous debate. When we imagine being a DRO owner and attempting to sell our services to a community, we challenge and break the mental habits of evasion or compliance to authority.

By far the most popular video that I have ever produced has been an off-the-cuff discussion of how best to approach a job interview. This video explicitly follows anarchic principles, in so far as I remind people that although they are being interviewed, they are also the ones doing the interviewing, and evaluating the person who is evaluating them. In the same way, when you are on a first date, if you only worry about how you are being perceived, rather than being curious about how you are perceiving the other person, then you are not in fact having a relationship at all, but rather are acting out an empty form of self-erasure and compliance to the needs and preferences of someone else.

When you explore the anarchic paradigm of human interactions, you continually imagine sitting on the other side of the negotiating table and attempting to provide benefits to yourself.

In the statist paradigm, we struggle to exist under a coercive and one-sided monopoly. We never practice sitting on the other side of that table, because there is no other side to that table, any more than slaves get to negotiate their wages. We seethe with resentment or hysterical "Stockholm Syndrome" patriotism, but we no more think of *reasoning* with our political masters then we think of trying to control a plane psychically while jammed in the back of "economy class."

When we are on the receiving end of brutal and coercive instructions, our self-esteem, our very *souls*, fade and flicker and diminish and collapse. We cannot think of ourselves fundamentally as having value because we are never treated as if we have value in and of ourselves. Our teachers seem constantly irritated with us, our parents are constantly correcting and managing us, and our preachers are constantly informing us of our sins.

Self-esteem has a lot to do with believing (or at least understanding) that we have value in and of ourselves, and that our feelings and thoughts are worthy of consideration. We are treated so little this way when we are children that I strongly believe that we grow up fundamentally scarred in our ability to comprehend our own independent value.

For instance, I can only remember one incident in my childhood when I was able to sit with an adult and chat in a relaxed fashion – and be asked questions – for any length of time. It was with a camp counselor, when I was 13 or so. I couldn't sleep, and we sat out front of our cabin, looking up at the stars, and chatting easily back and forth about our thoughts. (I clearly remember him telling me that everyone thought Frankenstein was the monster, when in fact it was the name of the doctor who created him – and I know that I remember that for very clear reasons, to do with my family! For anyone who is interested, I used that interaction as the basis of the sleepover conversation between the two girls in my novel "The God of Atheists.")

When we repeatedly picture the natural "win-win" interactions of an anarchist society, we unconsciously remind ourselves that we are worthy of being negotiated with, and that other people have to bring value to the table if they want to interact with us – that we do not exist simply to fulfill the greedy needs of others.

This mental exercise has staggering benefits in our personal relationships – and is the surest and most stable set of bricks that we can use to build a bridge to the future. Once we get used to the idea that we are worthy of negotiation, and that other people need to bring value to our lives in order to be of value to us, our self-esteem necessarily rises proportionally.

I face this quite often in my conversation with people in a variety of forums, including the Freedomain Radio Board. People will be difficult, or negative, or hostile, or evasive – and *genuinely believe* that I have some duty or obligation to continue to interact with them.

This is fundamentally a statist position, insofar as these people do not believe that they have to provide consistent or overall value in order to receive resources from others. In the past, before I became an anarchist and practiced this way of thinking, I was very susceptible to this kind of entitlement and manipulation. Now, however, it has become almost funny for me to see the shock that people experience when I simply find interacting with them more negative than positive. Almost inevitably, they will attempt to "rope" me in by attempting to snag me with my own values ("I thought you valued debate!") – or, if I ban them for being genuinely unpleasant or abusive, they haughtily inform me that I am "censoring" them, and going against "anarchism," and rejecting the values I proclaim *on my very website* ("free") and so on.

The truth of the matter is that I am acting in complete accordance with anarchistic principles when *I refrain from interacting with people who do not bring me value*. The fact that they are unable to "sit on the other side of the table" and empathize with my perception of the interaction only tells me that they have a long way to go in the journey towards understanding what voluntarism really means. The idea that I – or anyone – "owe" them any form of interaction is entirely statist in its essence. It is the belief that value does not have to be reciprocal, that one side can dictate terms to the other – and, most fundamentally, and most subtly, that the "values" of the person *not* receiving value should force them to continue the interaction. ("Don't you love your country?")

When we get used to sitting on both sides of the table, so to speak, it becomes that much harder to exploit us, and press us into the service of other people's neurotic defenses, needs and desires. We get habitually used to "checking in" with our own feelings, to see whether or not we are enjoying a particular interaction – and if we are not, we feel perfectly free to disengage. We do not "owe" other people time, energy or resources – they must "earn" our attention through positivity, just as an entrepreneur must "earn" our business through the provision of value.

When we raise our standards in this manner, it is certainly true that large numbers of people will react with incomprehension (and sometimes hostility), because we are in a very real sense rewriting our social contract with those around us. Before, they could count on us to provide them with what they wanted, and they did not have to trouble themselves by considering what *we* wanted. When we begin to require reciprocity in our relationships, people tend to get upset with us, because we are in fact highlighting their own entitled narcissism.

To give a minor example, as you may know I give listener conversations for free over the Internet, which I then publish as podcasts if the listener agrees. The majority of people politely request these conversations – however, a not-insignificant minority simply inform me that they are "ready" for a conversation. This is always surprising to me, the idea that I somehow "owe" them a conversation, because I am "dedicated" to philosophy and mental health. (This entitlement is all the more jaw-dropping when these people tell me in advance that they do not want to this conversation released as a podcast – and don't even offer to donate either!)

Helping people to understand that they need to provide value in their relationships is a very tricky and challenging endeavor – but one that is vastly easier with people who have genuinely and deeply explored anarchism and voluntarism, particularly in their own personal relationships.

Once people understand that if they do not provide value in their relationships, they do not in fact *have* relationships, but rather are just using people in an exploitive manner, then they can work to undo the damage of the legacy that they have inherited from their family and their school and their church, which is that you either take value from people, or you give value to people – but a *mutual* exchange of value is not possible. You either steal, or you are stolen from – this is not the best paradigm for having a strong, deep and emotional understanding of the "free market of relationships" that is the primary characteristic of an anarchic world view.

Thus, exploring anarchy will free you in your world *right now*, the world you actually live in, the world of your professional, familial and social relationships. Learning how to negotiate from both sides of the table will make you a more powerful and effective employee; a better and more loving spouse; a happier and more credible parent – it will bring you all the joys and liberties of a free society, even as you labor under excessive taxation and regulation.

Finally – and not insignificantly – the more that we can teach people, directly or by example, that relationships must be mutually beneficial in order to be considered positive, the more we will teach people that the State is evil, because it is one-sided, and violent, and exploitive.

The world will be free of the State when we finally see that the State is inferior to *all* of our personal and professional relationships. When we are completely used to thinking in terms of mutual advantage, the violent exploitation of the State will finally become clear to us, and it will fall away.